THE ARITHMETIC OF LIFE AND DEATH

George Shaffner

Ballantine Books
New York

A Ballantine Book
Published by The Ballantine Publishing Group

Copyright © 1999 by George Shaffner

All rights reserved under International and Pan-American
Copyright Conventions. Published in the United States by The
Ballantine Publishing Group, a division of Random House, Inc.,
New York, and simultaneously in Canada by Random House of
Canada Limited, Toronto.

Ballantine and colophon are registered trademarks of
Random House, Inc.

www.randomhouse.com/BB/

Library of Congress Catalog Card Number: 00-193407

ISBN: 0-345-42645-2

Manufactured in the United States of America

Cover design by Drew Pennington-McNeil

First hardcover Edition: September 1999
First Trade Paperback Edition: January 2001

10 9 8 7 6 5 4 3

For Grace, our children, and their children

Contents

Acknowledgments

I wish to thank the following for their instrumental contributions to *The Arithmetic of Life and Death:*

- Anya Karavanov, for her diligent research;
- Bill Brastow, for checking and rechecking the calculations;
- Pat Brown, for being the devil's advocate in the details;
- Jane Dystel, my agent, for having the courage to take me in;
- Cheryl Woodruff, my editor, for slapping me around; and
- Grace, for listening to it all, over and over, without (much) complaint.

Preface:
The Refugees from Math

". . . and the different branches of arithmetic—
Ambition, Distraction, Uglification, and Derision."

—LEWIS CARROLL

The Arithmetic of Life and Death began by accident in 1997 when I noticed a change in my octogenarian mother-in-law. Normally a cheerful, bright woman, her mood began to darken as her brother-in-law, also in his eighties, slowly lost his fight against cancer and its complications. Certainly, my mother-in-law was sad for him and for her older sister. But there was something else gnawing at her from within. For the first time in her life, she was afraid of dying. Though a devout, lifelong Catholic, she was afraid because she wasn't absolutely sure that there was another life waiting for her on the other side of this one.

Not the spontaneous hugging sort, I decided to write "Life after Death," a brief essay that uses common sense, along with rudimentary chaos theory and a little inferential logic, to establish a secular case for life after death. I do not claim to have cracked the mystery of the ages, but my mother-in-law seemed to feel a lot better after she read it.

If a little chaos could help my mother-in-law believe in life after death, I dared to believe that a little arithmetic could help my twenty-year-old son understand why he was involved in motor vehicle mishaps with such consistency. The result was a short, arithmetic essay called "The Odds of Getting Caught." The speeding tickets stopped. That success inspired "The Value of Education," which compares the career earnings of a high school dropout, a high school graduate, and a college graduate using earnings data from the U.S. Bureau of Labor Statistics. My son finished high school.

Shortly thereafter, a personnel problem at work motivated me to write "Prima Donna Effect" and "Teamwork," both of which use simple arithmetic models to show why people have to work together. My success in implementing the lessons learned from those two essays later prompted the writing of "Common Cause" and "Why More Things Go Wrong," by which time *The Arithmetic of Life and Death* had taken on a life of its own.

As the chapters increased in number, I began to discover that many of my relatives, a few of my friends, and practically all politicians seem to live their lives in a sort of innumerate bliss—a state in which virtually all remnants of mathematical thought have been exorcised since high school. These people are the "Refugees from Math."

Now is not a good time to be a Math Refugee. This is the Age of Information; numbers are everywhere: time and temperature, height and weight, speed and distance, power and capacity, prices and discounts. Principal, interest, taxes, and insurance. Dealer prep, transportation, licenses, and fees.

All of these are numbers. They represent information that is different from words. Each and every one of them can be applied, analyzed, and manipulated—especially manipulated—in thousands of ways that words can't.

It is important to preserve this distinction between words and numbers. For example, although the word *ten* can be subtracted from the word *twenty*, the result is the rather difficult to express *wty*. And even if it were possible to settle on a standard pronunciation, it might be somewhat harder to agree on how to multiply *wty* by eleven. For similar reasons, it was essential that Roman numerals, which look exactly like letters of the alphabet, were replaced by the distinctive and elegant Arabic number system sometime prior to the creation of NASA. (Skeptics and the "innumerati" should consider a simple example, such as dividing MMCCLXV by CCCLXIII, before appealing the matter to the Roman Catholic Church.)

Astronauts and rocket scientists notwithstanding, there seem to be a lot of Math Refugees out there. How else can one explain tailgaters, who cause one-sixth of all traffic accidents in return for getting to work about two seconds sooner (from "The Tailgater's Advantage")? Or teenagers who leave high school just before their senior year, when a diploma could be worth half a million dollars more to them in future income (from "The Value of Education")? Or that coworker (and every office seems to have at least one) who apparently feels no personal obligation to perform actual work (from "Why You Must Produce")?

These aren't nickel-and-dime mistakes. They are limb-threatening, self-impoverishing, or employment-ending errors. None of them should be made by someone who understands how to apply arithmetic to everyday problems.

Plain old arithmetic. Differential calculus, number theory, finite geometry, and every other form of advanced mathematics are not at all necessary. That is because every discipline of mathematics is constructed on the four corners of arithmetic: addition, subtraction, multiplication, and division. Intelligent application of these four simple tools, which everyone understands, can solve almost any problem.

Except one. Every year in every high school, when the last bell rings after the last class of Algebra II, in a moment of unrestrained group euphoria, the Refugees from Math shut down their left brains, and another small exodus from math begins.

After twenty-eight years of paternal observation, eighteen years of math and statistics education, and a day or two of nostalgic reflection, I concluded that the continuing exodus from math remains rooted in the way that it has always been taught: too much abstraction, too much symbolism (the equations), too much complexity, too much rigor (all those proofs!), and lessons that were and are too damned long. Thus, the design criteria for *The Arithmetic of Life and Death* became: Use real-life examples, use actual words and numbers, keep it simple, keep it short, and exterminate all equations with unknown stuff in them (okay, there's one in "Are We Alone?").

Each chapter of this book is intended to explain some facet of life that can best be understood with the help of arithmetic. To keep the book within the realm of the real, most of the chapters use everyday examples extracted from the unfolding stories of a family or two from the Pacific Northwest. Although the characters are fiction, their challenges are not. There is something for every Math Refugee:

- For impending adults: "The Odds of Getting Caught" and "The Value of Education";
- For graduates and newlyweds: "Investing Young" and "Personal Debt";
- For the compulsive: "The Case for Smoking" and "Gambling";
- For the indecisive: "The Sum of All Decisions" and "The Gift of Fallibility";
- For problem employees: "Why You Must Produce" and "Teamwork";
- For managers: "Consensus at Work," "Common Cause," and "MB(U)O";
- For aspiring politicians: "The Duke of Pork" and "Figures Don't Lie . . .";
- For the terminally cheerful: "The National Debt" and "Death by Misadventure";
- For mystery buffs: "Are We Alone?" "Streaks and the Law of Averages," and "Coincidence";
- For the elderly: "The Importance of Small Infinities" and "Life after Death";
- For the paranoid: "Why More Things Go Wrong" and "A Message from Rapa Nui."

Although an accident in the beginning, *The Arithmetic of Life and Death* ultimately evolved into a book that explains what to do in modern times. With the gracious assistance of the Sharpes and the DeNialls, those fictitious but prominent families from the Northwest, it also explains why, in everyday arithmetic.

THE
ARITHMETIC
OF LIFE AND DEATH

PART

I

Multiple Choices

"It's not that easy bein' green."

—KERMIT THE FROG

The Probability That You Would Be You

*"What is the odds so long as the fire
of soul is kindled . . ."*

—CHARLES DICKENS

Since some six billion people now occupy planet Earth, one could conclude that human life is as common as dirt in Denmark. There is, however, some evidence to the contrary. Gwendolyn Sharpe, anthropology student, and daughter of a prominent Northwestern personality, is a good example.

Like every human being, Gwendolyn is a construction of forty-six chromosomes. Twenty-three came from her mother, Cecilia, and the other twenty-three came from her estranged father. Each of her parents had forty-six chromosomes from which to choose, nicely organized in twenty-three pairs. Through the miracle of natural selection, either one of each chromosome pair from each of her parents could have been chosen for production. The resulting twenty-three chromosomes from each parent were then paired to make Gwendolyn's forty-six.

The odds that Gwen would get the exact twenty-three chromosomes that she received from her mother were one-half times one-half times one-half times one-half, a total of twenty-three times, or .5 to the twenty-third power. That means that the probability that Cecilia would give Gwendolyn the twenty-three chromosomes she got was about one in ten million (10,000,000), which was less likely than winning the state lottery (about one in seven million in Washington, although the odds are longer in some states).

The odds that Gwen would get the twenty-three chromosomes she got from her father were also about one in ten million. So, the probability that Gwendolyn would be Gwendolyn was about one in 100 trillion (one in 100,000,000,000,000). On any given day, a win in the Washington state lottery would be around fourteen million times more likely than a Gwendolyn Sharpe.

But that assumes the existence, union, and productive sex lives of Gwen's mother and father. Gwendolyn's parents met at a small Pacific Northwest university with a student population of 1,000 men and 1,000 women. Like so many young women back then, Gwen's mother hoped to meet and marry the man of her dreams before leaving college with a degree in accounting. Like so many young men back then, Gwendolyn's father planned to practice a few of the more physical rituals of marriage throughout the six years it would take him to obtain an undergraduate degree in political science. Correctly assuming, however, that Gwendolyn's mother would inevitably prevail, the maximum probability of the productive union of her parents was a one-in-a-thousand long shot, which lengthened the odds of Gwendolyn's existence to about one in 100 quadrillion (1 in 100,000,000,000,000,000).

However, the odds of Gwendolyn's mother's being her mother were at least one in 100 quadrillion, too. The probability that her father would be her father was the same. So the odds of Gwendolyn's being Gwendolyn were closer to one in 1,000,000,000,000,000,000,000,000,000, 000,000,000,000,000,000,000,000,000. But that figure excludes consideration that either parent might have been infertile, that either might have been killed before conception, or that they might have divorced before the moment of magic that produced Gwendolyn or any of her brothers. Nor has there been any inclusion of the extreme unlikelihood of the existence of Cecilia's parents, who were from Yakima and Chewelah, or her husband's parents, or their parents, or their parents, ad infinitum.

Netting all of this down to scientific terms, the odds that Gwendolyn would be Gwendolyn were less than one in a jillion gazillion. The same is true for each of us. Against such long odds, every life is a miracle of immeasurable proportion, courtesy of nature. Thus, the existence of so many billions of people is not evidence of the commonness of life but a testament to the infinite scale of nature's benevolence.

Acceptance of such an improbable gift is not without obligation. An annual donation to the National Wildlife Fund is sweet, but the gift of life requires payment in kind. In order to fairly compensate nature for her generosity, each of us must help others to enjoy the gift, we must never harm or take the gift from another, and we must each live our own life to its fullest extent, despite the inevitable bumps in the road.

You Can('t) Be Anything You Want

"Not every soil will bear all things."

—VIRGIL

At one time or another, most American children are told that they can be anything they want to be. The message is an American tradition; the traditional messengers are good-hearted parents, grandparents, aunts, and uncles. What they mean is that the United States is a land of great opportunity, which is true. But young children, who have yet to compare American economic, social, racial, and religious obstacles to those that exist in other nations, don't always get the intended message. Instead, what the children may actually hear is that they really can be anything they want to be—which is not true and never has been.

Gwendolyn Sharpe, a very fit twenty-year-old at five foot two and 105 pounds, is never going to play defensive end for the Green Bay Packers. She's too small. Even though he loves to race, Billy Ray DeNiall, who at age sixteen is already six foot three and 190 pounds, is never going to ride a Triple Crown winner. He's too big. Although he loves airplanes, Joe Bob DeNiall, who is Reginald's older son, never had a chance to be a Naval fighter ace. He is color-blind and has 20/400 vision.

Clearly, there are physical criteria for many professions. No one is born with a physique that can meet them all. In fact, the physical requirements for occupations such as defensive end and prima ballerina are mutually exclusive.

There's also a scarcity problem. Many thousands of Americans, if not millions, may have aspired to the presidency of the United States. But in the 210 or so years that the office has existed, there have been only forty-one of them. As enticing as it may seem nowadays, the solution is not to shorten the term of the presidency to one day (even though such a change would have allowed some 76,000 more Americans to live the dream).

The scarcity problem exists, to a somewhat lesser extent, for all of the highest-paying and most exciting jobs such as congressman, Fortune 500 CEO, and major league baseball player. On any given day, there are around 435 of them, 500 of them, and 750 of them, respectively, a total of 1,685 as of the 1999 baseball season. But there were also around 139,000,000 million Americans in the workforce in 1999, which is more than 82,000 times 1,685.

This means that everyone cannot be anything they want to be. There isn't room. If there were, we would be a nation of politicians, presidents, and pitchers, and nobody would be doing any real work.

Since all of the best jobs are scarce, they are also competitive. This is where the land of opportunity comes into play. In the United States, almost anyone, providing he or she meets any pertinent physical criteria, can compete. But the scarcer the job, the tougher the competition.

Joe Bob DeNiall, for instance, may have poor eyesight, but he envisions himself as the CEO of a major U.S. company by the time he is forty years old, which will be in the year 2020. Since there are about 2,500 American companies with more than 5,000 employees today; assuming only 2 percent annual growth, there ought to be as many as 3,900 by 2020.

However, according to the Census Bureau, there will also be some 322 million Americans in the year 2020. If 51.3 percent of them are employed (as there were in 1998), then there will be more than 165 million workers in theoretical competition with Joe Bob. Even if only half of them will have had enough experience to be selected for a CEO slot, that would still appear to leave Joe Bob's odds of success at about one in 21,000 or so (82.5 million ÷ 3,900), which seems like a bit of a long shot, even for a congressman's son.

Joe Bob knows, however, that many of today's CEOs have master's degrees in business or a related area. So Joe Bob plans to get an M.B.A. from a top-notch business school by the year 2005. If he does well, he is also certain that he can get a good job with a large company that favors advanced education. If his new company grows to 20,000 employees by the year 2020, then it might appear that Joe Bob's chances of becoming CEO by then would be right around 1 in 20,000.

In itself, that doesn't appear to be much of an improvement over 1 in 21,000. But Joe Bob knows that only about 7 percent of Americans get any sort of advanced degree and that only about 20 percent of those are degrees in business. Even if Joe Bob's company employs twice that many, Joe Bob's chances should improve to around 1 in 560 ($20,000 \times .07 \times .20 \times 2$).

After that, Joe Bob will just have to outperform the remaining competition. It will help—a lot—if he has a talent for the job.

At some point in their youth, the most successful people choose a career that fits one or more of their talents. This means that they avoid those professions where their ability to compete may be hampered. Stevie Wonder, a genius musician and songwriter, would have been less successful as an art critic. And it is unlikely that Alan Greenspan, economist extraordinaire, advisor to presidents, and the head of the Federal Reserve, would have had similar success high kicking with the Rockettes.

But effort is even more important. American history is full of examples of extraordinary people who overcame handicaps with persistence. George Patton, a West Point graduate and one of the greatest field generals in American military history, had a serious learning disability. Muggsy Bogues, at five feet, three inches tall, became a starting guard among giants in the National Basketball Association. And Stephen Hawking has overcome the debilitation of Lou Gehrig's disease to become the world's leading astrophysicist.

If Joe Bob is a talented manager, and especially if he works hard at it, he may succeed in becoming a major company CEO. Approximately 3,900 talented and hardworking individuals will be just that in the year 2020. But even if Joe Bob fails, he may still have a successful career. If his future employer has 20,000 employees, then at least 50 of them are likely to be executives one or two levels below the CEO, including COOs, CFOs, CIOs, subsidiary and division presidents, general managers, executive vice presidents, senior vice presidents, and even everyday, garden-variety vice presidents.

Relative to the number of CEO jobs at Joe Bob's company, that's a fairly big safety net. It could improve Joe Bob's chances of "executive suite" success to perhaps 1 in 11—if he gets the M.B.A., if he has the talent, if he works hard, and if he can accept a definition of success that is something less than the pinnacle.

"Alice's Restaurant" is not real life. You can't be anything you want. It's not a right guaranteed by the Constitution. But if you aspire to something extraordinary, you do have a better opportunity in today's United States than in any other nation on Earth at any time in history.

The Value of Education

or

How to Earn $200 per Hour in High School

*"Educated men are as superior to uneducated men
as the living are to the dead."*

—ARISTOTLE

Every year, thousands of bored, underperforming, or dis-
enfranchised teenagers drop out of high school prior
to graduation, even in the idyllic Northwest. Billy Ray
DeNiall, who at age sixteen is not at all like his ambitious
older brother, decided to quit school at the conclusion of
his sophomore year. Like most conscientious parents, his
father vehemently disagreed, which instantly resulted in the
usual shouting match.

After the elder and junior DeNialls managed to calm
down, Billy Ray agreed to go to the library and check
out the 1996 publication of the U.S. Department of
Labor's Bureau of Labor Statistics. In it, he discovered that
college graduates earned an average of $719 per week, high
school graduates earned an average of about $450 per

week, and those who did not complete high school earned about $318 per week.

Therefore, ignoring inflation, an average college graduate will earn about $1.495 million over a forty-year career. High school graduates can work longer. Over a forty-four year career, they should average $1.03 million dollars in earnings, some 31 percent less than college graduates. Those who don't complete high school should work for about forty-six years and will earn just under $760,000 on average, 26 percent less than high school graduates and 49 percent less than college graduates.

Graduates make a lot more money. But there is a price: all that extra school.

Billy Ray needs two more years to get his high school diploma. At 180 days per school year and a diligent eight hours per day including study time, that is a total investment of 2,880 hours. If Billy Ray becomes an average wage earner, he will make about $270,000 ($1.03 million minus $.76 million) more as a high school graduate than he will if he drops out. That is a return of $135,000 for each of his last two years of high school, or more than $93 for every additional hour of class and homework ($135,000 ÷ 180 × 8).

Using the same assumptions of eight working hours per day and 180 days per school year, the cost of college is another 720 days or 5,760 hours of hitting the books. The return, however, is an additional $466,000, about $116,500 per year, or more than $80 per hour of college—and more than fifteen times minimum wage.

However, these figures presume no inflation, which

is implausible as long as there is a Congress.* Assuming that the starting salary is one half the career average in each category and inflation is 5 percent from 1997, then career earnings for the year 2005 college graduate will be around $3.68 million for forty years of work, $2.37 million for the year 2001 high school graduate over forty-four years, and $1.7 million for the high school dropout over a forty-six-year career that starts on the first day of the year 2000. (For those of you keeping score, the model assumes that each graduate begins work on January 1 of the year after graduation.)

This means that Billy Ray's extra two years to finish high school are likely to be worth about $675,000, or about $337,000 per year and $234 per hour—which is more than some lawyers make! If he can keep his focus for another four years of college, his bachelor's degree should be worth another $1.31 million, or more than $325,000 per year. Try making that kind of dough at the local pizza franchise.

Graduate school (a master's degree or a Ph.D.) is also financially attractive. In 1996, people with advanced degrees averaged nearly $48,000 per year. Equalized against the other examples, a graduate with an advanced degree will earn about $1.77 million in 1996 dollars over a thirty-seven-year career and about $4.59 million assuming 5 percent inflation.

---

* According to the U.S. Bureau of Labor Statistics, the last full year in which there was no U.S. inflation was 1954 during the Eisenhower administration. The last time there were two consecutive years of no inflation was 1938 and 1939 under Franklin D. Roosevelt. Since 1954, there have been 44 consecutive years of inflation.

The four levels of academic achievement compare economically as follows:

Academic Level	1996 Income	Career Length	Career Earnings	Earnings/Hour Staying in School
No Diploma	$16,536	46 years	$1.70 million	N/A
Diploma	$23,400	44 years	$2.37 million	$234/hour
Bachelor's Degree	$37,388	40 years	$3.68 million	$227/hour
Advanced Degree	$47,944	37 years	$4.59 million	$212/hour

Money isn't everything, but, like knowledge, having more of it is demonstrably superior to having less of it. The highest paying job most folks will ever have, Billy Ray included, is school: more knowledge; more money; win-win. Therefore, the only intelligent decision is to stay in school until graduation. Any other course is too likely to lead to a lifelong, low-budget search for what might have been.

Less knowledge equals less money and lower self-esteem. Lose-lose-lose.

4

The Sum of All Decisions

"When you come to a fork in the road, take it."

—YOGI BERRA

Gwendolyn Sharpe, daughter of Cecilia, never had any doubts about whether she would go to college. From an early age, she knew she would. But as graduation from high school approached, and as the pressure to decide mounted, the question of which college to attend became more and more difficult.

Like many ambitious high school students, Gwendolyn had applied to a large number of universities. In fact, she had applied to twelve, all highly regarded. Because she was an excellent student with very good S.A.T. scores and because she required no financial aid, she had been accepted by nine of them. After a lot of research, hours of debate with her friends, and several consultations with her school counselor, she had managed to narrow the field of candidates to five.

But now, in the final days of her high school career, a decision was overdue. Yet Gwendolyn, who intended to major in anthropology, felt paralyzed because there was no clear winner: The best academic university was also the most expensive, the college with the best school of anthropology was the second-most expensive, the university with the best overseas research program was in the middle of a large and expensive northeastern city, the university closest to home had a weak anthropology program, and the least expensive choice was a small school in a small town with nonexistent prospects for employment.

As Gwendolyn's deadline approached, she found she had no alternative but to ask her mother for assistance. Cecilia, in turn, managed to stifle her surprise and immediately agreed to help. Once they had cleared away the dinner dishes that night, the two of them sat down to see if they could resolve the dilemma. First, Cecilia listened to Gwendolyn's analysis of the situation at length, which was an excellent example of proper teen parenting. Then she went into the kitchen to fix the two of them a cup of coffee. In the meantime, she asked Gwendolyn to get a few pages of graph paper and a pencil. Gwen was puzzled, but since she was also suffering from digestion-induced oxygen deprivation in the brain, she decided not to question her mother this one time.

When they got back together at the table, Cecilia took charge of the pencil and paper and asked Gwen to list what was important to her in the selection of the right university. After lengthy discussion and an idea or two from Cecilia, Gwen agreed that the most important selection criteria were: university reputation, quality of the anthropology curriculum, future employment prospects, tuition cost (one of Cecilia's suggestions), living costs (another from Cecilia), opportunity for postgraduate work, quality of student life, closeness to home, and quality of student living facilities.

Next, Cecilia asked Gwendolyn to rank each of the five universities, one criterion at a time, with five being the best score and one being the worst. After a lot more discussion, and no small amount of reconsideration and alteration, Cecilia was able to produce a simple table of Gwendolyn's rankings:

	School #1	School #2	School #3	School #4	School #5
University Reputation	5	4	3	2	1
Anthropology Curriculum	4	5	3	1	2
Future Employment	3	4	5	2	1
Tuition Cost	1	2	3	4	5
Cost of Living	2	3	1	4	5
Postgrad Research	3	4	5	2	1
Quality of Life	5	1	2	4	3
Closeness to Home	3	2	1	5	4
Student Living Facilities	3	4	2	5	1
Totals	**29**	**29**	**25**	**29**	**23**

Gwendolyn and Cecilia were both happy to have such a clear picture of the situation, but given the lateness of the hour, both were also disappointed that three universities were still in the running. So Cecilia suggested that Gwendolyn apply a weighting factor to the remaining three universities that would tend to emphasize the most important criteria and de-emphasize the least important. After some discussion, they agreed to multiply the most important three criteria by a factor of three and the next three most important criteria by a factor of two. While Gwendolyn watched hopefully, Cecilia produced the following result (with five still being the highest score before weighting):

	School#1	School#2	School#4
Triple Weighted (most important)			
University Reputation	15	12	6
Anthropology Curriculum	12	15	3
Future Employment	9	12	6
Double Weighted (average importance)			
Tuition Cost	2	4	8
Cost of Living	4	6	8
Postgrad Research	6	8	4
Single Weighted (least important)			
Quality of Life	5	1	4
Closeness to Home	3	2	5
Student Living Facilities	3	4	5
Totals	**59**	**64**	**49**

At this point, Gwendolyn understood her dilemma. She had preferred the first university for its excellent academic reputation and the fourth university for its quality of life, but the second university was clearly the best combination of quality education and reasonable cost. Cecilia was happy to agree. And they were both relieved to have such an important decision behind them.

As she neared the completion of her undergraduate degree in anthropology four years later, Gwendolyn found herself in a similar quandary, this time over which postgraduate assistantship to accept. On this occasion, Gwendolyn brought the paper, the pencil, a Sharp (no relation) calculator, and the work she had already done, which had reduced the original six offers by half. However, there appeared to be no difference in the remaining three:

	Offer #1	Offer #2	Offer #3
Triple Weighted			
Opportunity for Research	9	6	3
Salary & Benefits	3	9	6
Quality of Teaching Staff	6	3	9
Double Weighted			
Academic Reputation	6	2	4
Cost of Living	6	2	4
Opportunity for Overseas Fieldwork	2	6	4
Single Weighted			
Size of Classes	1	3	2
On-Campus Living Facilities	2	3	1
Closeness to Home	1	2	3
TOTALS	36	36	36

The first university had the best research program and an excellent reputation in Gwen's field of study, but the compensation package was poor and it was far from home. The second university had the best compensation and living facilities, but it had poor lab facilities and a mediocre teaching staff. The third university had a renowned staff and was close to home, but the best research positions were already filled. Once again, Gwendolyn was in a dilemma, and the weighted ranking system had not managed to clarify the situation.

Cecilia reviewed Gwendolyn's work carefully, asking many

questions in the process. After ascertaining that the table was a fair and reasonable illustration of the situation, Cecilia suggested that Gwendolyn replace the original ranking system with a relative system using ten as the highest score. Then the other two offers would each be given comparative scores of zero to nine depending upon their relative merit versus the top-ranked criterion, which would, once again, tend to amplify gaps in preference. Gwendolyn agreed and, with a little help from Cecilia at the calculator keys, quickly produced a revised table:

	Offer #1	Offer #2	Offer #3
Triple Weighted			
Opportunity for Research (10,9,8)	30	27	24
Salary & Benefits (7,10,9)	21	30	27
Quality of Teaching Staff (8,7,10)	24	21	30
Double Weighted			
Academic Reputation (10,4,9)	20	8	18
Cost of Living (10,4,9)	20	8	18
Opportunity for Overseas Fieldwork (6,10,9)	12	20	18
Single Weighted			
Size of Classes	7	10	9
On-Campus Living Facilities	8	10	7
Closeness to Home	5	7	10
TOTALS	**147**	**141**	**161**

Although she could not be certain that the third university would turn out to be the best one, Gwendolyn was sure that accepting its offer was the best decision for the moment. Cecilia concurred and, since Gwendolyn had just turned twenty-one, offered to open a bottle of wine to celebrate. First, though, she asked Gwen to decide between an excellent chardonnay, a new white zinfandel, and Cecilia's personal favorite, Chablis.

Gwen, who was an inexperienced drinker, did not know which one to choose. After some deliberation, however, she decided to take a calculated risk on the chardonnay.

The Value of Being Stupid

"You pays your money and takes your choice."

—PUNCH

W hen we are young, parents and teachers spend a lot of time teaching us how to make thoughtful, intelligent decisions. Once we have money, though, the circumstances reverse and it becomes important for us to be stupid.

Joe Bob DeNiall, Billy Ray's older brother and the eldest son of Reginald, unexpectedly encountered exactly such a situation shortly after qualifying for his first credit card when, freshly outfitted with unprecedented wealth, he decided that he absolutely had to have a new, more powerful stereo. So, on an otherwise ordinary afternoon, he jumped into his pickup and drove right down to his local, multimedia entertainment superstore to check out the latest in sound systems for the home. Even Joe Bob, who prided himself on his knowledge of current technology, was surprised to find so many choices. In fact, there were more than 100 stereo models on display produced by more than twenty different manufacturers, which varied in cost from less than $100 to more than $3,000.

Joe Bob found himself practically paralyzed by opportunity. Fortunately, however, there was a helpful salesperson on hand who, after learning that Joe Bob recently had been granted the instantaneous ability to borrow up to $3,000 without parental consent, was more than happy to spend as much time as necessary to ensure that her new acquaintance make an informed decision.

Joe Bob, who had been taught to pay attention in school, listened carefully while the salesperson explained all the important features of the latest new stereos and why the best equipment cost the most money. After no more than a few minutes, however, Joe Bob found all of the terminology, all of the acronyms, all of the various features, and all of the different choices more than a little bewildering. And all of the stereos sounded terrific. So, having also been taught that it was important to seek professional advice on complex matters, Joe Bob asked the salesperson which stereo was the best buy for the money.

Sensing his discomfort, the salesperson immediately pointed out a powerful little number that cost only $2,000 and which was personally endorsed by a famous rock star. She added that, because of its popularity, there were only a few of them left, that it was a thousand dollars less than Joe Bob had to spend, and that, if he bought the stereo that day, it would be shipped directly to his home for free. Thrilled that he had finally found the best stereo and relieved at not having to drive his new acquisition home on the flatbed of his pickup in the rain, Joe Bob quickly consummated the transaction.

Three days later, after uncrating and assembling the stereo in his room, Joe Bob invited his father and younger brother in for a demonstration featuring Pink Floyd. Billy Ray was mightily impressed, but Reginald, although he approved of the musical selection, was not. Instead, he left the room and quickly returned with several consumer magazines devoted to audiophiles, who are people that are abnormally interested in sound reproduction.

Joe Bob, who had just become a heavy investor in stereo technology, read the magazines that night. Unfortunately, he quickly learned that his new stereo had recently finished last in a comparison test of six similar systems in the same price range. He also read that a new, more powerful, more reliable, and less expensive model would soon replace his and, therefore, most retailers were heavily discounting the obsolete system that he had just bought at list price.

At that moment, Joe Bob swallowed his pride and admitted to himself that he had made the wrong choice. Unfortunately, since the boxes had been trashed and since the transaction had taken place three days earlier, the sale was final and there was no way that he could return the stereo.

That decision was bad for Joe Bob. Ironically, however, it was not necessarily bad for the economy. From an economic point of view, in fact, it would be difficult to overstate the importance of large quantities of hasty and uninformed decisions.

We live in an era of diversity. Thanks to globalization and the strength of the U.S. economy, we, like Joe Bob, are often faced with an unprecedented array of choices. In general, choice is beneficial to the consumer and at the very core of competition. But there is also a downside. It is that, regardless of the number of options, there can be precisely one superior choice. All of the other alternatives must be, therefore, relatively inferior.

In the long run, consumers benefit from the fact that a plurality of buyers make the right buying decisions. That means that the manufacturer of the best product gets the largest share of the market and, therefore, that the focus of competition remains, at least to some extent, on producing the best possible product.

However, only one manufacturer stood to gain from Joe Bob buying the best stereo. Therefore, at that moment in time, it was in the interest of the other nineteen stereo manufacturers that Joe Bob make an error.

Thus, at a microeconomic level, it generally can be said that the majority of the supply side gains from an inferior decision. It is, in fact, an arithmetic certainty in any market where there are three or more competing suppliers,* as follows:

Number of Competitors	Number of Best Products	Number of Inferior Suppliers	Number Gaining from Bad Decisions	Percent Gaining from Bad Decisions
3	1	2	2	67%
5	1	4	4	80%
7	1	6	6	86%
10	1	9	9	90%
20	1	19	19	95%
50	1	49	49	98%

* When there is a single supplier in any given market, or when there is a single dominant supplier, then a condition called monopoly exists and the government steps in to restore competition. Once competition is restored, so is the opportunity for *buyer* error, although it may also be said that monopoly is the only market condition that guarantees it.

Although all reputable manufacturers strive to build the best product, and although many attempt to divide the market into smaller chunks (called segments) in which their products may be more favorably viewed, most manufacturers are aware that they may not always succeed. In addition, the majority of manufacturers believe that buying decisions are far more emotional than logical. As a result, much of their advertising is dedicated to inducing the consumer into an emotional, rather than informed, decision. The most common methods include:

1. Icon association, which means that a famous person, by virtue of his or her willingness to promote a specific product, therefore implies its superiority. Of course, the icon is usually paid large sums of money to deliver this message, which may induce icon bias.

2. Emotional appeal, wherein the promoter of the product equates something of emotional importance to the purchase decision: Fashion = belonging or coolness or sex; cosmetics = love or sex; food = approval or sex; cars = envy, stature, freedom, or sex.

3. Implied superiority. In complex markets, almost any producer can find some facet of its product, even if it is singular and somewhat unimportant, which is superior to at least one highly regarded competitor. The manufacturer will then use the promotion of this relative superiority as a basis upon which to imply general superiority of the entire product. (This is called generalizing from the particular, which is a logical fallacy and, therefore, endlessly employed by both business and government.)

4. Free goodies. With the exception of new product in-

troductions, whoever has the worst product has to give away the most stuff so that people will buy it. The giveaways, of course, are worth a lot less than the cost of the product. Otherwise, it would be cheaper to throw the product away if it couldn't be sold.

These mechanisms, and many others, are not just designed to induce the buyer to make an inferior selection. They are also intended to motivate consumers to buy more than necessary, to do it frequently and, if necessary, to borrow to keep up. That is because, the more often consumers consume, and the more often they err, the better the economy performs. So, to a *large* extent, the health of the economy depends upon bad buying decisions.

Although the health of the economy should be important to you, it is not a responsibility that you should take personally. Instead, you should endeavor to be part of the plurality of consumers who buy the best products and, therefore, force inferior manufacturers to improve their offerings in order to survive.

Joe Bob, however, was both poorly informed and unfortunate to get an experienced salesperson. As a result, he fell to Icon Association (endorsement = superiority), Emotional Appeal (expensive stereo = coolness), and Free Goodies (free = good). He wasn't alone. These days, almost all markets are besieged by large quantities of suppliers, which means that lots of buyers must be making inferior decisions.

Economists have a lot of politically correct labels for this condition, such as buy side suboptimization, market inefficiency, and satisficing, just to name a few. They all converge on the same arithmetic certainty: In diverse markets, which is practically all there are in the industrialized world, the majority of suppliers benefit from a lousy decision. Therefore, the weight of advertising and sales is bound to promote stupidity.

If you are uninformed, like Joe Bob was, then you are vulnerable to making a wrong decision, like Joe Bob did. To a large extent, the odds will be against you because the majority of manufacturers will benefit from your error, so they will attempt to induce it via known advertising and sales techniques. Therefore, once you become a consumer, it is your responsibility, and solely your responsibility, to ensure that you are well enough informed to make a sound buying decision.

The Gift of Fallibility

"Love truth, but pardon error."

—VOLTAIRE

Reginald DeNiall, Billy Ray's father and a Washington (the state) representative to the United States Congress, is both a talented politician and a student of the electoral college. He knows that every piece of proposed legislation possesses the potential for political suicide. So Reginald, who is not a trained statistician but who is thought by some to covet a seat in the Senate, decided in his first year in office that he would never support any bill unless he was at least 75 percent certain that his vote would reflect the wishes and desires of his core constituency—the top ten contributors to his election campaign.

Convinced that he had found a way to minimize any risk of future campaign funding deprivation, Reginald began to vote when 75 percent confident, or to abstain when less so, on each new legislative proposal. Unfortunately, even at 75 percent assurance per bill, Reginald's probability of avoiding a mistake for just three consecutive votes was .75 times .75 times .75, which was less than 43 percent. And his chances of making as many as five correct decisions in a row, even though each individual vote was heavily weighted in his favor, were less than one in four (about 23.7 percent).

True to form, Reginald soon made a mistake that inflamed the antipathies of his benefactors. Being nothing if not career minded, Reginald instantly concluded that he had to revise his strategy. Since no elected official can abstain on all but five bills over two years and still get reelected, except in Louisiana, a draconian reduction in voting activity did not appear to be a viable long-term solution. So Reginald chose another alternative. He subscribed to every on-line library and polling service, he tripled his research staff, and he demanded from all of his advisors and consultants a 90 percent likelihood of voting correctness.

If his recently enlarged staff are on their toes, then Congressman DeNiall's current chances of error on any individual vote are now very small—only one in ten. Once again, though, the long run is against him. By Reginald's seventh ballot, the odds favor at least one mistake, and the probability that he will make one or more mistakes in the next twenty-five votes is almost 93 percent.

History suggests, rather strongly, that elected officials may make a few more mistakes than one in seven. And, of course, politics has never had much to do with real life. Medicine, however, does have to do with real life, and doctors, in particular, are plagued by the inevitability of error and its consequences. The number of things that can go wrong with a human being is, after all, infinitely large. But the time available to determine the cause of a life-threatening illness or injury is never infinite, meaning that, in some cases, certain death will precede certainty of diagnosis.

In life-threatening situations such as these, we don't want to require doctors to wait until they are 100 percent sure of the cause. The patient will die first. So we want to empower doctors to make an enlightened guess whenever necessary. In return, however, we must live with the inevitability of error, as they must, even though the consequences may be dire.

In fact, we all must make choices, so we all must make mistakes. (Decision avoidance theorists may wish to read the afterword, "Why More Things Go Wrong" before arguing the point.) That is because there are times when all of us will be forced to make decisions prior to knowing all of the facts, all of the consequences, or all of the alternatives. Even if we could be as much as 95 percent certain of every decision we make, we would still be likely to make at least one mistake by only the fourteenth decision. At only five decisions per day, 95 percent probability of making the right decision every time would still result in nearly two mistakes per week, more than ninety mistakes per year, and about 7,000 mistakes in an average lifetime.

But nobody has the luxury of being 95 percent certain with regularity, and most folks have to make more than five decisions per day. So mistakes are a fact of life. More important, some mistakes are living evidence of the courage to make tough decisions. That means that we must not only extend the Gift of Fallibiity to ourselves, we must also learn to graciously accept the well-intended mistakes of parents and role models, spouses, and children, friends and family, including in-laws, subordinates and peers, and bosses (yes, even bosses). The Gift of Fallibility need never extend, however, to the habitual repetition of dangerous error.

The Case for Smoking

"Habit, n. A shackle for the free.*"*

—AMBROSE BIERCE

More than 400,000 Americans die from cigarette consumption every year. That's the city of Austin, Texas, up in smoke, each and every twelve months. But one in five American adults still smokes, even in Austin, and the habit is on the rise among teenagers.

Most get hooked up with cigarettes in their youth. It's hip, it's a duty-free method of adult behavior simulation, and it's cheap. Bought in bulk, cigarettes still cost only fifteen cents or so, or about three cents a minute.

But most smokers get hooked for the long haul. That's because smokers discover, even after they become genuine adults, that it is very difficult to quit (more than three out of four fail). So the costs tend to accumulate.

Billy Ray DeNiall, Reginald's youngest son, started smoking earlier this year at the advanced age of sixteen.

Desperate to simulate the fullness of adulthood, he already smokes a pack and a half a day. If his habit stays the same, he will spend more than $80,000 on cigarettes by the age of sixty-six—at today's prices. But if inflation averages 5 percent over the next fifty years, then the long-term cost of Billy Ray's habit will exceed $340,000.

In order to spend $340,000 on cigarettes, Billy Ray will probably have to earn around $490,000 (assuming a marginal income tax rate of 30 percent, the other $150,000 or so will go to various and sundry governments in the form of income taxes). So unless he can quit, Billy Ray's pack-and-a-half habit is likely to cost him an average of $9,800 per year, which is more than $25 per day, over the long haul.

A Corvette is likely to be much cheaper—and a lot less dangerous. The rule of thumb is that Billy Ray's life will be shortened about one minute for every minute he smokes, or about an hour and a half per pack. So if he sticks to his habit of a pack and a half a day for the full fifty years, then his death will be hastened by four to five years. That may not seem like a lot to a sixteen-year-old, but it will loom rather larger at the age of sixty-six. In the meantime, Billy Ray will be sick more often, he will have less strength and stamina, and, up close and personal, he will smell like a wet yak.

Smoking is the archetypal drug habit. It is extraordinary in the beginning, then ordinary, then necessary, then addictive. Over the long run, it is destructive to life. Each and every cigarette is a promissory note—a habit-forming commitment to pay as much as one-third of a million dollars to the tobacco farmers, the cigarette manufacturers, the cardiovascular surgeons, and the morticians who trade in its wake.

Billy Ray is not alone in his vigorous support of this important industry. One in five Americans still smokes. More than 400,000 die every year from complications caused by the habit. If there are 1,000 people in your circle of friends and acquaintances, then about 160 of them will die before their time from cigarettes.* That is 160 funerals that you should plan to attend, unless you also smoke, in which case you should be planning your own.

* According to the U.S. Census Bureau, one American dies every thirteen seconds. That equates to 277 deaths per hour, 6,646 deaths per day, and around 2,427,000 deaths per year. If 400,000 Americans die every year from the effects of cigarette smoke, then approximately 16.5 percent of all deaths result from the habit, which is 165 out of every 1,000.

The Odds of Getting Caught

"But from each crime are born bullets that will one day seek out from you where the heart lies."

—PABLO NERUDA

For most popular offenses, the odds are against getting caught. That's why they're popular. But offenders still manage to get caught with remarkable consistency. If it weren't for teenagers, this might be a mystery.

Billy Ray DeNiall, Reginald's youngest son and a second-year entrepreneur at the local high school, believes he is an undiscovered Formula One racing talent who needs to exercise his aptitude on a regular basis. So he drives his Dodge pickup truck at a steady fifteen miles per hour over the speed limit to and from school every day.

The local police, who are understaffed, can allocate only one car to patrol the roads leading to and from the high school. Since it is a large high school, there are so many roads, and there is so little time, the police can apprehend an average of only one in every hundred high school speeders on any given patrol.

Billy Ray is a keen observer of local law enforcement in action. He knows that he has only a 1 percent chance of getting caught on any given trip and just a one-in-fifty chance of getting caught in any given day. So he speeds with confidence and consistency.

But the school year is 180 days in length. Unless Billy Ray mends his ways, he will be ticketed an average of 3.6 times per school year, a total of ten or eleven tickets in his three years to graduation. The fines will be substantial, Billy Ray's already stratospheric insurance rates will escape Earth's gravitational influence, and his license may be revoked.

The same principle holds for more serious forms of illegal activity. Although the odds may be against getting caught any one time, the chances accumulate with repetition. Also, since law enforcement officials are sensitive to taxpayer opinion, the odds of getting caught tend to increase with the severity of the offense.

If, for example, the chances of robbing a bank without getting caught are 75 percent, then one would expect three out of four bank robbers to be on the loose. But thieves never rob just one bank, because a single crime hardly adds up to a productive career. Besides, the odds are always against getting caught the next time.

Let's suppose that a career in bank theft requires about one robbery every four months or so. Then, even at a 75 percent probability of success per theft, the chances of avoiding apprehension are less than 32 percent by the fourth heist ($.75 \times .75 \times .75 \times .75$). Thus, more than two bank robbers in three will celebrate their first anniversary on the job in jail. After two years, just one in ten bank robbers will still be plying the trade, which is why there are more felons in jail than there are on the street.

According to local law enforcement officials, in fact, 90 percent of all bank robbers in the Puget Sound area are apprehended. One ought to seriously question the sanity of any career that offers a 90 percent attrition rate after only a few paydays, much less one that results in a multi-year engagement at the local penitentiary shortly after apprehension.

The odds of getting caught also hold for legal but potentially lethal activities. If the chances of having unprotected sex without contracting a social disease are 90 percent per encounter, then the odds of making it an extracurricular hobby, say one new rendezvous per month through two consecutive years of junior college, are less than 8 percent. That means that the odds of at least one disease transmission, the consequences of which may be fatal, are more than 92 percent. Using the same 90 percent probability of avoidance per monthly conquest, the odds of contracting one or more sexually transmitted diseases will exceed 99 percent prior to the completion of a four-year bachelor's degree.

An informed sense of statistical mortality can also be useful in career planning. If, for instance, your chances of successfully squeezing an extra $200 out of your monthly expense report are 98 percent, then you might expect to increase your income by $2,400 per year with impunity. However, by the thirty-fifth month, your odds of getting caught will exceed 50 percent. In that period, you will have "made" an extra $7,000. But the consequences of getting caught are likely to include immediate termination. If your salary is $48,000 per year, and if it takes you six months to find an equivalent job, then your net loss, excluding humiliation, will be $17,000 ($24,000 in salary less $7,000 in improperly claimed expenses), which is 85 times $200 per month.

Arithmetic is a hard master. It will punish anyone who believes that a pattern of mistakes or unnecessary risks is a series of isolated, one-time occurrences. America's graveyards are full of dead people who thought they could make a career out of repetitive stupidity. America's jails are full of living people, currently 1.5 million of them, who thought that they could make a career out of crime. America's streets are full of unemployed people who thought they could make a career out of not working.

With repetition, the odds of getting caught always move rapidly toward certainty. It is a Law; there are no exceptions. Including you.

PART

2

Division of Labor

"O, how full of briers is this working-day world!"

—WILLIAM SHAKESPEARE

Why You Must Produce

*"The engine which drives Enterprise
is not Thrift, but Profit."*

—JOHN MAYNARD KEYNES

Most forms of human endeavor consume money. Some consume lots of it, especially government. Only one form of human endeavor produces money, which is commerce. In this regard, the business of commerce is very important, because it pays for everything else.

Before any business can pay for anything else, however, it must pay for itself. This means that each and every enterprise must cover its own costs for people, facilities, equipment, transportation, and outside services. Whatever is left over after all of its internal costs have been covered is called profit. Usually, the company keeps some of its profit for future investment, pays some to the government in the form of taxes, and returns the rest to its investors in the form of dividends.

Investors create companies. No company has ever been

started without at least one of them. All investors have the same objective: to get back more money than they originally invested. Alternatively, no investor has the objective of getting back less money than originally invested. That would be like investing in Congress, which would be absurd were it not required by law.

If a business is not profitable, by the way, it will not be able to pay all of its bills. Then, in order to keep itself alive, it will eventually require an injection of new capital, which means additional investors. These new investors will not commit more capital to the company without the expectation that they will eventually get more back than they invest.

So every business must be profitable or it will eventually fail. The responsibility for the profitability of the business is shared by its employees, who are paid solely on the expectation that this promise will be fulfilled.

Since the responsibility for making money is shared by all of the employees of a company, it might be easy for any individual to assume that the responsibility is not personal. But such an assumption is a form of theft, because it steals the time and effort of all of the other employees who must unfairly shoulder the lost portion of productivity. Usually, those who do not shoulder their fair portion of the workload are not employed for long.

The size of each individual's burden may not be intuitively obvious. These days, an average employee costs one and a half to two times basic salary. The rest of the money is for the plant or office, furniture, telephones, fax machines, computers, insurance, many taxes, and many, many other expenses. So an employee who makes $40,000 per year in base salary actually costs the business $60,000 to

$80,000 per year by the time all of the other expenses are added up. But this level of production produces no profit. If the business is to make a 10 percent profit after taxes, it must produce a pretax profit of about 15 percent (about one-third of business profits are consumed by taxes). This means that the productivity burden on each $40,000 employee is actually from around $70,500 to about $94,000, or 1.8 to 2.4 times base salary.

Cecilia Sharpe, Gwendolyn's mother, works in a small, 24-person, professional accounting firm where the average salary is $45,000 per year. The average annual cost per employee is $81,000, or 1.8 times salary. This means that the company must produce $1.944 million in revenue (24 employees × $81,000) to break even. In order to make a 10 percent tax profit, it must produce $2.16 million, or $90,000 per employee per year.

The company must produce $2.16 million in revenue regardless of how many of the 24 employees actually pitch in. If, for instance, two employees at the firm (such as the aunt and uncle of the managing partner) are completely unproductive, then the burden on the other 22 employees climbs to more than $98,000 per year. To produce that much more, each employee will have to work almost 9 percent harder, which is more than a month of extra work per employee. As you might expect, the affected employees are unlikely to be enthused. So the managing partner will be expected to correct the productivity problem, even if it is in the family.

Return on investment is not an arcane economic theory or some artificial number that large companies bandy about in the press. It is a principle that is at the heart of free enterprise, and it is a prerequisite for the ongoing transaction of business. Moreover, the principle of return on investment applies to each employee in every enterprise. If you take a company's money in salary and other forms of compensation, then it is your responsibility to produce more than what you cost so that your employer may be profitable.

In the former Soviet Union, there used to be a common saying among the proletariat that went, "We pretend to work, they pretend to pay us." But that was a communist society, so it was okay to pretend to work, at least until 1989 or so. Ours, however, is a capitalist society, so it is against the law for your employer to pretend to pay you. If you pretend to work in America, therefore, you must either be a politician or you will be out of a job.

Focus on Priorities

"The heavens themselves, the planets, and this center
Observe degree, priority, and place . . ."

—WILLIAM SHAKESPEARE

In these quality-focused, service-centered, megahertzed times, many businesspeople are faced with a never-ending barrage of new tasks. The conscientious attempt to squeeze in as much work as possible. Personal productivity, however, is frequently less dependent on the zeal of the squeeze than it is on the intelligence of it.

Faced with an unknown quantity of randomly arriving work, most people resort to one of three methods of work organization:

1. They attempt to complete each task in the order it arrives (called FIFO in industry argot, which means first in, first out).

2. In order to minimize the number of tasks left in the

"In" basket at the end of the day, they do the easiest ones first.

3. Because the hardest tasks are the most difficult to predict and complete, they get them out of the way first.

Each method has its advantages and disadvantages, and each produces a different result.

Coincidentally, Cecilia Sharpe encountered exactly those three methods of organizational behavior when she was consulting at a local bookkeeping firm. In order to determine which of the three methods was most productive, she created a series of eight tasks, each with a different degree of difficulty and varying economic value to the firm, as follows:

Order of Arrival	Time to Complete	Billable Value
1)	90 minutes	$120
2)	120 minutes	$150
3)	15 minutes	$25
4)	60 minutes	$50
5)	30 minutes	$100
6)	105 minutes	$200
7)	75 minutes	$180
8)	45 minutes	$75
Totals	540 minutes	$900

To simulate real-world behavior, Cecilia put all eight tasks, which were unrelated to each other, on the desk of each of three bookkeepers at the beginning of the workday. She told each of them that any uncompleted task was not billable and therefore would not contribute to the day's productivity. Finally, she told each of the bookkeepers that they had only five hours to complete as much work as possible because a two o'clock meeting had been scheduled in the controller's office to discuss travel policy, which would take up the rest of the day.

Well aware that a nine-hour workload for a five-hour day was typical of their company's management style (see chapter 18), the three bookkeepers approached their tasks with stoic resolve and their usual methodology:

1. The first bookkeeper performed each task in order of arrival. After five hours, she had completed tasks 1 through 4 and was halfway done with the fifth. Since work-in-progress was not billable, her daily contribution to the firm was $345.

2. The second bookkeeper, a small, black-haired, spark plug of a woman named Helga, always wanted to complete as many tasks as possible. As a result, she finished five tasks: numbers 3, 5, 8, 4, and 7. She also managed to complete 83 percent of task number 1, but it didn't count. Her total contribution to the firm was $430.

3. The third bookkeeper attacked each task in the order of difficulty (greatest to least), finishing only tasks 2 and 6. His total productivity was $350.

It appeared to Cecilia, and to her client's controller, that the method of doing the most tasks was best. But the next day, just to make sure, Cecilia reversed the order of arriving tasks and asked the first bookkeeper to repeat the test. Taking each task in order of arrival, she managed to complete numbers 8, 7, 6, and 5, producing a total of $555 in billable revenue. This proved to be a substantial victory for her method and a point of some embarrassment for Cecilia, Helga, and the local management team.

Cecilia, however, was undeterred. She went home that evening, sat down with her Sharp (no relation) calculator, and reanalyzed the problem. The solution began to come clear when she restructured the task list as follows, by equalizing all tasks to value per hour:

Task	Length	$ Value	$ Value/Hour
5)	30 minutes	$100	$200
7)	75 minutes	$180	$144
6)	105 minutes	$200	$114
3)	15 minutes	$25	$100
8)	45 minutes	$75	$100
1)	90 minutes	$120	$80
2)	120 minutes	$150	$75
4)	60 minutes	$50	$50

Cecilia returned to work the next day and asked Helga, the second bookkeeper, to perform the tasks in the order of productivity, meaning highest value per hour. After five hours, Helga had completed tasks 5, 7, 6, 3, and 8 for total billable productivity of $580, which was 4.3 percent to 68 percent more productive than every other method that had been tried. And she had an extra thirty minutes left over to help the controller write up the new travel policy.

Having solved the problem to management's satisfaction, Cecilia moved on to her next consulting assignment. But when she returned a few months later for the annual audit, she was surprised by what she found. Despite the best efforts of the controller, the first and third bookkeepers had persisted in their simple but suboptimal ways. Helga, however, had adapted her work behavior by prioritizing her projects based on value. As a result, she had received a promotion to cost accountant, a merit raise, her own office with real wood furniture, and the veiled antipathies of the two bookkeepers left behind in the catacomb of cubicles at the other end of the hall.

During the audit, Cecilia and Helga had plenty of time to chat. Over the course of their conversations, they both agreed that they had learned three things:

1. In today's business world, the amount of work always exceeds the amount of time available to get it done.
2. Those who prioritize by value to the business will be most successful.
3. Despite the obvious benefits of value-based prioritization, most workers will persist in completing tasks by order of arrival or degree of difficulty.

In the end, Helga and Cecilia both concluded that this state of affairs, although counterintuitive and backward, was an opportunity for those willing to adapt, to focus, and to prioritize. They also agreed to tell only their close friends and coworkers.

Rules of Thumb

"Any excuse will serve a tyrant."

—AESOP

In life, there seem to be a lot of "Rules of Thumb." In general, Rules of Thumb are guidelines people invent to explain phenomena that they can't prove. If these rules seem to work, then other people use them and they eventually become widespread, perhaps too much so. One of the more popular Rules of Thumb is the "80/20 Rule," which is very arithmetic and which suggests, for instance, that 20 percent of teenagers will get 80 percent of the tattoos, or that 20 percent of your guests will drink 80 percent of your wine, or that 20 percent of your customers will be responsible for 80 percent of your business.

When Cecilia Sharpe first joined the accounting firm where she still works to this day, she noticed that there was an enormous gap between the salaries of a few of the firm's top employees and the rest of the staff. So Cecilia, who was responsible for the company payroll, approached the managing partner on the issue. That is when she discovered that he was a devotee of the 80/20 Rule of Thumb. More specifically, he ascribed to the theory that 20 percent of his employees produced 80 percent of the company's results and that, therefore, a geometric gap in salaries was more than justified.

Intuitively, Cecilia had a hard time accepting such a large disparity in either pay or performance among peers. In order to explain her intestinal discomfort to both herself and the boss, she created a simple "cotton picking" model:

1. Suppose that ten cotton pickers picked 100 bales of cotton;
2. Then, according to the 80/20 Rule, the top two pickers picked eighty bales of cotton; and
3. The bottom eight pickers picked only twenty bales of cotton.
4. So the top two pickers produced an average of forty bales each; but
5. The bottom eight pickers produced an average of only 2.5 bales each;
6. Which means that the top two pickers were sixteen times as productive as the bottom eight pickers (40 ÷ 2.5)!

Although impressed with Cecilia's imagination, the managing partner remained unmoved. To make his point, he wagered one dollar that Cecilia would find that the 80/20 Rule was, in fact, a reasonable reflection of real-world employee productivity.

Cecilia accepted the wager. However, since companies

that measure productivity tend to keep their results confidential, she had a difficult time finding a general but statistically rich business model in which individual productivity could be analyzed within a framework of overall performance.

After more discussion with the managing partner, Cecilia finally agreed that professional sports, which were statistically rich at both the individual and team level, would provide a fair and reasonable basis for their test. That very Sunday, while surfing the Net, she came across the 1997/1998 statistics for the now defunct Seattle Reign professional basketball team. The eleven scorers for the Reign that season were:

Player	Total points
Enis	754
Whiting	645
Starbird	557
Paye	300
Aycock	269
Ndiaye	195
Holmes	195
Smith	93
Godby	73
Hedgpeth	85
Orr	89
Total	**3,255**

If the 80/20 Rule was correct, Cecilia should have been able to predict that the top two scorers, Shalonda Enis and Val Whiting, who composed 18.2 percent of the team's personnel, would have produced nearly 80 percent of the points. However, they scored only 1,399 points, which was just 43 percent of team production. When Cecilia added in the production of the number-three scorer, Kate Starbird, then 27.3 percent of the players produced a little more than 60 percent (1,956 or 60.1 percent) of the team's point total for the year.

Even though the Reign's results were far removed from 80/20, there still seemed to be a large gap in personal productivity. In addition, Cecilia was certain that her boss would not accept the results from a women's team, even if the sports model was his idea. So she logged on to her favorite Internet portal and searched out the 1997/1998 statistics for the Seattle Supersonics basketball team. That year, their fifteen players scored as follows:

Player	Total Points
Baker	1,574
Payton	1,571
Schrempf	1,232
Ellis	932
Hawkins	862
Perkins	580
Kersey	234
Anthony	419
Williams	298
McMillan	62
McIlvaine	247
Cotton	24
Wingate	150
Zidek	29
Howard	25
Total	**8,239**

The top 20 percent of the Supersonic's scorers, who were Vin Baker, Gary Payton, and Detlef Schrempf, produced 53.1 percent (4,377) of the points. In comparison, the top five scorers, who were 33.3 percent of the team, were responsible for 74.9 percent of the team's total point production.

Thus, although the 80/20 Rule seemed to be in error, it began to appear to Cecilia that there might be some basis for a 70/30 Rule, or maybe a 60/30 Rule. However, even this seemed like more of a productivity gap than could be naturally explained, so Cecilia decided to research relative player production in each of several other statistically important categories in basketball:

Team	Percent	Points	Rebounds	Assists	Steals	Blocks
Reign	Top 27%	60%	57%	59%	51%	71%
Supersonics	Top 33%	75%	69%	81%	68%	82%
Average	Top 30%	67%	63%	70%	59%	76%

Overall, the top 30 percent of the team in each category produced about two-thirds (67 percent) of the results. Before presenting her findings to the managing partner, though, Cecilia decided to test two other team sports. In baseball, Cecilia found that the top 30.4 percent of the Seattle Mariners in each batting category (excluding all pitchers) produced 70.4 percent of the runs, 69.9 percent of the hits, 78.2 percent of the home runs, and 74.4 percent of the runs batted in. In hockey, Cecilia found that the top 30 percent of the Vancouver Canucks were responsible for 65.8 percent of the goals and 59.4 percent of the assists.

Balancing performance across all four teams produced the following results:

Team	Top Percent	Average Productivity
Reign	27.3%	59.6%
Supersonics	33.3%	75.0%
Mariners	30.4%	73.2%
Canucks	30.0%	62.6%
TOTALS	**30.2%**	**67.6%**

When confronted with the numbers, the managing partner had to conclude that the 80/20 Rule was probably invalid, at least when applied to employee productivity. But Cecilia had to concede that it was only a slight exaggeration from the more accurate, but less assonant, 67/30 Rule. While he reached into his wallet for a one-dollar bill, Cecilia restructured her "cotton picking" model:

1. Again, ten cotton pickers picked 100 bales of cotton;
2. But, according to the 67/30 Rule, the top three pickers picked sixty-seven bales of cotton; and
3. The bottom seven pickers picked only thirty-three bales of cotton.
4. So the top three pickers produced an average of 23.33 bales each; but
5. The bottom seven pickers produced an average of only 4.714 bales each;
6. So the top three pickers were still 4.9 times as productive as the bottom seven pickers (23.33 ÷ 4.714)!

Although happy to win the bet, Cecilia still found the result bothersome. In all of the sporting cases, the star players had substantially more playing time than the rest of the team, which must have skewed raw productivity in their favor. But in business, she noted, practically everyone worked the same forty- to sixty-hour workweek.

Once again, the managing partner disagreed. In his opinion, giving the most time to star players was the definition of good management and any deviation toward equality of opportunity was certain to cause overall team productivity to plummet.

Fearful that the managing partner might use the 67/30 Rule as an excuse to downsize the business, Cecilia asked for time to revisit personal productivity by equalizing opportunity for all of the players on each team. The managing partner was happy to accept her offer—but double or nothing on the original bet if overall productivity fell by 10 percent or more after equalization, since even such a small dip would erase the profitability of many businesses.

Equalized Opportunity

". . . a fair chance, in the race of life."

—ABRAHAM LINCOLN

Despite the "discovery" of an improved 67/30 Rule of Thumb (from the previous chapter), Cecilia was convinced that inequality in opportunity had distorted the productivity gap between players on the teams that she had researched. So, with a firm lack of support from her managing partner, she returned to her sports models in search of resolution.

First, Cecilia decided to equalize the 1997/1998 playing time of all of the players on the roster of her once favorite but now obsolete basketball team, the Seattle Reign. Since the eleven members of the team had played a total of 8,850 minutes in their one full season, it was a simple matter to adjust every player's point production as if each had played exactly 804.5 minutes each. When she did, the player productivity picture changed remarkably:

Player	Total Points Before Equalization	Total Points After Equalization
Enis	754	454
Whiting	645	375
Starbird	557	304
Paye	300	188
Aycock	269	211
Ndiaye	195	408
Holmes	195	214
Smith	93	276
Godby	73	356
Hedgpeth	85	204
Orr	89	157
Team Total	**3,255**	**3,147**

Contrary to even her own expectations, total Reign point production fell only 108 points, just 2.45 points per game. Although that might have been a significant factor in professional sports, it would have been no more than a simple 3.3 percent productivity drop in business, and one which might have been more than offset by a reduced dependence on "star" salaries.

In addition, the identity of the stars seemed to change somewhat after equalization: The top 27.3 percent of the team's shooters were Shalonda Enis, Astou Ndiaye, and Val Whiting, but they scored only 39.3 percent of the points, compared to 60.1 percent in the nonequalized model.

Next, Cecilia equalized the playing time of all fifteen Seattle Supersonics to 1,314.9 minutes each, producing the following:

Player	Total Points	Equalized Points
Baker	1,574	703
Payton	1,571	657
Schrempf	1,232	591
Ellis	932	632
Hawkins	862	436
Perkins	580	455
Kersey	234	429
Anthony	419	540
Williams	298	518
McMillan	62	292
McIlvaine	247	268
Cotton	24	956
Wingate	150	361
Zidek	29	596
Howard	25	620
Total	**8,239**	**8,054**

In the case of the Supersonics, team point productivity dropped by 185 points, or 2.2 percent, which was even less than the Reign. After equalization, point productivity of the top five players (33.3 percent of the team) was just 44.3 percent of the team total.

Cecilia then equalized performance for both the Reign and the Supersonics across the same five measurements that she used in her original analyses:

Equalized Opportunity Model

Team	Percent	Points	Rebounds	Assists	Steals	Blocks
Reign	Top 27%	39%	40%	42%	40%	67%
Supersonics	Top 33%	44%	42%	66%	52%	72%
AVERAGE	**Top 30%**	**42%**	**41%**	**54%**	**46%**	**69%**
Not Equal	Top 30%	67%	63%	70%	59%	76%

With the early results counted, Cecilia began to feel confident that something like a 50/30 Rule was a far more accurate representation of equal opportunity than 67/30 or 80/20. Further analysis tended to confirm her hypothesis.

After equalizing the 1997/1998 Mariners baseball team to 239.4 at bats each, Cecilia discovered that the team batting average dropped from .275 to .252 as the number of hits fell to 1,390 from 1,515, an 8.3 percent drop, and home runs fell from 239 to 163 (down 31.8 percent). But total runs scored, which was the most material measurement of team productivity, dropped only 2.9 percent, from 800 to 777. The effects of equalization on top player performance were also similar to her first two analyses, with the top seven (30.4 percent) Mariners producing 38.4 percent of the runs, 36.5 percent of the hits, 59.6 percent of the home runs, and 45.4 percent of the runs batted in.

Finally, Cecilia equalized opportunity for all of the hockey players on the 1997/1998 Vancouver Canucks to 82.4 shots on goal. As a result, total team goals fell from 193 to 182.7, a drop of 5.3 percent, but assists rose from 286 to 295.9, a 3.4 percent increase. After equalization, the top 30 percent of the team produced 38.2 percent of the goals and 46.8 percent of the assists.

Cecilia was led to two conclusions. The first was that, despite significant drops in secondary measures such as shots blocked and home runs, equalization of player opportunity had had a smaller negative effect on primary productivity measures than she had expected:

Team	Measurement	Productivity Drop
Reign	Points	3.3%
Supersonics	Points	2.2%
Mariners	Runs	2.9%
Canucks	Goals	5.3%
AVERAGE PRODUCTIVITY LOSS		**3.4%**

Cecilia's second conclusion was that, by equalizing opportunity, the 67/30 Rule had collapsed to a figure nearer to 47/30:

EQUALIZED OPPORTUNITY MODEL

Team	Top Percent	Non-Equalized Productivity	Equalized Productivity
Reign	27.3%	59.6%	45.5%
Supersonics	33.3%	75.0%	55.3%
Mariners	30.4%	73.2%	45.0%
Canucks	30.0%	62.6%	42.5%
TOTALS	**30.2%**	**67.6%**	**47.1%**

Before presenting her results to the managing partner and collecting her second consecutive dollar, Cecilia ran the equal opportunity numbers through her "cotton picking" model one last time:

1. Once again, ten cotton pickers picked 100 bales of cotton;
2. But, according to the 47/30 Rule, the top three pickers picked forty-seven bales of cotton; and
3. The bottom seven pickers picked fifty-three bales of cotton.
4. So the top three pickers produced an average of 15.667 bales each; but
5. The bottom seven pickers produced an average of 7.571 bales each;
6. So the top three pickers were still more than twice as productive (2.06 times) as the bottom seven pickers (15.667 ÷ 7.571)!

Later that evening, after a stimulating debate with the managing partner, an enriched but exhausted Cecilia had time to reflect on the previous few days. Although she suspected that years of additional analysis would lead her to the same controversial conclusions, she knew that she had proven nothing. But Cecilia also believed that she had learned several lessons:

1. That Rules of Thumb, like all generalities, should be applied with care;*

* Personal productivity has inherent limits, such as the similarity of the workweek, which, in the final analysis, make the 80/20 Rule a relatively poor predictor of productivity distribution. However, there are other, less limited statistical conditions where the 80/20 Rule may be more useful. For instance, it may be that as much as 80 percent of a company's business does come from only a fifth of its customers, especially if its customers are other companies and a few of them are much larger than the others.

Similarly, it is also possible, but not at all wise, that 20 percent of your less prudent guests may drink 80 percent of the wine at your next Super Bowl party.

2. That the star system may be inferior to equalized opportunity in many cases and may help explain, for instance, the phenomenal success of the 1998 New York Yankees; but

3. That, even in an environment of equalized opportunity, the best still appeared to be twice as productive as the rest—excluding considerations for cost.

It was the true accounting of the cost of the doubly productive that would soon return to haunt Cecilia Sharpe.

Prima Donna Effect

*"Do you know that all of the great work
of the world is done through me?"*

—CARL SANDBURG

Prima donnas are atypically productive personnel who may negatively impact the performance of people around them. Cecilia Sharpe's accounting firm recently hired such an employee. Nicknamed "the Whiz," he was adept at all forms of accounting. He could reconcile receivables, post payables, and repair errors faster than anyone in the firm. He was a magician at math and statistics. He was even a good financial analyst, and he worked very hard. Every senior manager in Cecilia's firm believed that the Whiz was twice as productive as any of the company's other accountants.

Not surprisingly, the Whiz shared management's enthusiasm for his personal performance. The center of his own universe, he had little patience for the less adept, which was everyone else. To his peers he complained about the direction of the company, the performance of management, and the insufficiency of his compensation. To management he complained about the direction of the company, the performance of his peers, and the insufficiency of his compensation.

Over time, three of the younger accountants began to emulate the Whiz. Meanwhile, others became disenchanted with the Whiz and his growing entourage. The office became polarized. People began to talk. Morale sank. Productivity fell.

At the request of the managing partner, Cecilia looked into the problem. Naturally, she took an accountant's view. Over the course of a number of auditing engagements, she studied the productivity of all of the firm's accountants. She found that the Whiz really was twice as productive as the company average. But, because of divisiveness, sinking morale, and rumormongering, she also found that the productivity of everyone else in the firm, including the three young accountants, had dropped by 5 to 15 percent each.

Using Cecilia's findings, the managing partner forecasted the firm's net change in productivity for the coming year. Although the Whiz would be worth two man years by himself, the rest of the company would lose a total of 2.4 man years (24 employees times an average productivity loss of 10 percent each). Thus, the Whiz's net contribution to the firm would be negative in aggregate (2.0 minus 2.4)!

Being an accountant himself, the managing partner could see little reason to pay any employee who actually reduced the overall performance of the firm. The Whiz was terminated the next day. The three young accountants were put on probation. Cecilia was assigned the responsibility of replacing the Whiz.

Cecilia eventually hired an average accountant named

Cal. Being mediocre, Cal had no ego to speak of. But he was a good listener, a good follower, a diligent worker, and a reliable volunteer. Whenever he was assigned to an engagement, the overall productivity of the team improved substantially.

Cecilia later determined not only that the overall performance of the company had been restored to its previous level but that, because of Cal's team attitude, it had increased another 5 percent. Thus, Cal's net contribution to the company was the equivalent of 2.2 man years (Cal's one year plus 24 times .05) compared to a negative 0.4 for his predecessor, a net gain of 2.6 man years.

Once again, the managing partner agreed with Cecilia's findings. He gave Cal a raise. Then, not being much of an astronomer, he made Cecilia's top priority the formation of a new plan to improve the performance of every other accountant in the firm by a similar margin. Cecilia, however, was both better read and a devotee of "The Discovery Channel," so she intuitively understood the cosmic nature of the problem.

From before the time of Christ until the Renaissance, it was generally believed that the sun and all of the universe revolved around planet Earth. That theory was, in fact, attributed to Ptolemy, who was the greatest mathematician of his time (circa A.D. 100) and who, to this day, remains accused of inventing trigonometry.

But the Ptolemaic Theory of the universe didn't work, as the Polish astronomer Copernicus later proved. The Ptolemaic Theory doesn't work in the universe of business, either. If, like the Whiz, you believe that the universe revolves around you, then your star is sure to fall.

Teamwork

*"We must all hang together, or assuredly
we shall all hang separately."*

—BENJAMIN FRANKLIN

How well you do your own job is critical to your future. But it will not be the sole determinant of your success in the workplace. That is because, like it or not, there are no tasks in either business or government that are done by individuals, especially big tasks.

When Joe Bob DeNiall, Reginald's elder son, is not studying at a nearby junior college, he is a machinist's apprentice assigned to the Boeing 777, a large commercial airplane that has about three million parts. The amount of time it takes to manufacture a 777 is a closely guarded secret. Not even Joe Bob knows how long it takes. But if each part can be designed, manufactured, tested, packaged, shipped, uncrated, unit tested, assembled, retested, flight tested, and flight retested (it is a passenger airplane) at an average of just ten minutes per part, then it takes around

30 million minutes to build a Boeing 777. That is an estimate of 500,000 man hours, or about 250 man years.*

If Joe Bob could do all of the work by himself, working eight hours per day for 250 days every year, then it would take him about 250 years to build one Boeing 777. But even if Joe Bob could live that long, it is unlikely that many of Boeing's airline customers could live with Joe Bob's delivery schedule.

On the other hand, if The Boeing Company were to assign 249 more professionals to Joe Bob's production team, then a new 777 airplane could be produced every year. Better yet, if a total of 6,000 personnel were assigned to the team, then a 777 could be produced every two weeks or so and the airlines could be afforded the opportunity to

---

* Approximation is imprecise by definition. Often, however, there is more than one path to the same estimation.

Before the acquisition of McDonnell-Douglas, The Boeing Company had about 100,000 employees who produced about thirty commercial planes per month. If 60,000 of them were devoted to the construction of new airplanes and the rest were employed in the maintenance of existing aircraft or in other Boeing businesses, then it would have taken about 2,000 man months (60,000 employees ÷ 30 aircraft per month) to manufacture a new commercial airplane. That is about 167 man years per plane. However, the Boeing 777 is a larger, more complicated airplane than the 737, which makes up the bulk of Boeing production. By multiplying the 167 man-year average by 1.5 to reflect the greater complexity of the 777, we reach the same 250 man-year result.

We can also approach the problem from an economic view. Suppose, for instance, that we estimate the selling price of each 777 to be about $150,000,000. By rule of thumb, we also assume that about 50 percent of the price is the cost to manufacture, which would be around $75,000,000. Approximately 60 percent of the cost to build is likely to be parts, and the other 40 percent is likely to be labor. So the cost of labor to build a 777 is around $30,000,000. If Boeing's fully loaded labor cost is around $60 per hour, then the total number of hours required to build a Boeing 777 is 500,000. Dividing 500,000 by 250 man days per year and 8 hours per man day (2,000) yields the number of man years estimated to build a 777, which, once again, is 250.

fly aircraft that are somewhat younger than their average traveler.

Almost all of us, especially the middle-aged and older, would prefer to fly in aircraft that were born after we were. The airlines, even most domestic carriers, are aware of our preference. Therefore, they insist on delivery schedules that are less than 250 years. Similar buy-side preferences exist in every other modern industry, although the supply side doesn't always seem to get the hint.

Last year, after a long day on the 777 assembly floor, Joe Bob decided to try a small, new Italian restaurant on his way home. Located near the Museum of Flight, it was called the Mayfly. The owner, it turned out, was a confirmed bachelor, an entrepreneur, and a gourmet chef. In addition, he was an aspiring industrial engineer who had determined that, at eight minutes per guest, he could personally manage up to fifteen concurrent diners at an average of two hours per meal. Since fifteen customers were more than he expected to serve in the Mayfly's early days, the restaurateur had decided to work as he lived—alone.

The moment that Joe Bob entered the Mayfly, the proprietor greeted him cordially at the door, seated him, and handed him a menu. He returned with a glass of water a few minutes later, but Joe Bob was not yet ready to place an order. Shortly thereafter, the owner returned to the table for a second time and Joe Bob selected the veal special.

While the restaurateur was making Joe Bob's Caesar salad, a nice young couple entered the restaurant. After pausing to thank the saints for so much luck on his first day, the restaurant owner stopped making the salad, washed his hands, and then went out front to greet the new arrivals. He then seated them at a table for two by the window and returned to the kitchen to get them each a glass of ice water. When he came back to their table, however, they weren't quite ready to order. So he stopped by Joe Bob's table to apologize for the slight delay, then returned to the kitchen to finish Joe Bob's salad. But, just as he was pouring the dressing, the man at the window called into the kitchen wanting to place the couple's order. So the restaurant owner rushed out of the kitchen with the Caesar salad, dropped it off at Joe Bob's table, then sprinted over to the window to serve the couple.

Just then, a family of five, including a small child, appeared at the front of the restaurant. So the sole proprietor finished taking the couple's order and hurried up front to meet the family of five. As he was seating them, Joe Bob asked for some bread and the couple by the window asked to see the wine list. Meanwhile, the father of the family of five requested a high chair and three children's menus.

While the proprietor was running for the children's menus, the wine list, the bread, and the high chair, four stevedores from the docks at Alki entered the restaurant looking hungry, thirsty, and large. The restaurateur, who had read neither "Streaks and the Law of Averages" (chapter 27) nor "Why More Things Go Wrong" (afterword), was caught off guard. But, being a man of action, he ran to the front of the store to greet the stevedores, who had been examining the beer list while they waited.

As soon as the four stevedores were seated, they asked for eight different microbrews and extra glasses so they could all share. At the same time, Joe Bob asked for his tea, which had not been delivered, and for his veal scallopini, which had not been started. Meanwhile, the couple asked for their bread and minestrone, and the father of the family of five asked for water for the children and a medium-priced Chianti for himself and his wife, and a plate of antipasto for the family to munch on while they waited.

At that moment, there were twelve guests in the Mayfly, which was only 80 percent of opening day capacity. It had been open for thirty minutes, which was just 2.5 minutes per guest and less than 30 percent of the carefully modeled eight minutes forecast. Yet, the restaurateur's single-server model had completely broken down. In a panic, he retreated to the kitchen to try to figure out what to do. Just as he was beginning to revise his service model to accommodate the chaotic arrival of multiple, mutually exclusive requests, a busload of tourists from the south side of Chicago squeezed into the front of the restaurant.

At that moment, Joe Bob, the couple, and the family of five got up and left, never to return. No one knows what happened to the proprietor, who seemed to vanish into thin air, but the rumor around Alki is that the four stevedores worked together to make the tourists a superb spaghetti Bolognese, and a good time was had by all in the Mayfly's final hour.

Whether it's restaurants or 777s or anything else, it's an interdependent world. Teams rule. There is no such thing as a sole proprietor—everyone relies on many suppliers. Even hermits depend on others to provide electricity, clothing, utensils, bedding, pens and paper, kitchen conveniences, packaged foodstuffs, and access to the Internet. Therefore, how well you get along will always depend upon how well you work with others, even if you choose to take a chance and work alone.

Why There Are Meetings

"All errors of consequence require collaboration."

—JULIAN DATE

To make teamwork work, there is a recurring need to coordinate: to determine near-term objectives, to checkpoint progress, to brainstorm difficult solutions, to change course, to make sure everyone has the same news. In many such instances, one-to-one communications don't always work. That is why meetings were invented. Many corporate veterans, however, believe that meetings are really a time-consuming management device that is used for the perpetuation of employee discord. For the sake of good morale, such beliefs should be examined from time to time, which is exactly what Cecilia Sharpe agreed to do just a short while ago.

At the time, Cecilia was managing an audit team of six accountants who were closing the annual books for two large customers. Between the pressure of their work at multiple customer sites and the usual office tasks, none of them felt they had the time to attend the hourlong progress meetings that took place every Friday. Cecilia, who has always been an excellent listener, agreed to eliminate the weekly meeting on an experimental basis in return for a commitment from each auditor to maintain direct communication with each and every other member of the team.

The very next Friday, Cecilia had to propose a revised work schedule to her auditing crew. Since they had fallen behind with one customer, the team had to decide whether to work ten hours per weekday until they caught up or to work Saturdays instead. Given the personal impact of the decision, Cecilia felt that each individual had to have the opportunity to voice an opinion and to hear the opinions of his or her peers.

Cecilia began to call the members of her team. She quickly discovered, however, that the probability of reaching any team member with one call was only 25 percent since there were several possible locations for each auditor, plus lunches, customer meetings, and travel between customer sites. Therefore, it took Cecilia twenty-four phone calls to reach all six members of the audit team.

The eighteen failed calls took only two minutes each. The six successful calls required an average of ten minutes each, during which time Cecilia and each accountant discussed the pros and cons of each proposal. At the end of the call, Cecilia asked that each auditor confer with each other before the end of business the following Tuesday, then get back to her with an opinion so that a timely decision could be made.

The next Monday, each team member commenced contacting each other. Because some were working in close proximity, they managed to reach each other by the second call, on average. It took only ten minutes per call for each member to have his say. By Tuesday afternoon, every team member had talked to every other and had gotten back to Cecilia for a ten-minute discussion of their individual recommendations, a total of twenty-one distinct communications.

For a variety of personal reasons, four team members favored working longer weekdays and two team members favored working on Saturdays. Although there was a majority opinion, Cecilia was certain that they would never accept a split result in a typical weekly meeting without more discussion. The next day, a Wednesday, she contacted each member of the team again, which took an average of four calls each. During ten-minute discussions, she requested that each member again confer with each other to see if a clearer decision could be reached by the end of the next day.

The team members repeated the process, then each contacted Cecilia by Thursday evening as promised. After a ten-minute update with each of them, Cecilia found that two team members had indeed changed their votes. Four members now favored working on Saturdays, and two members preferred longer weekdays.

Exasperated and out of time, Cecilia consulted with the managing partner. A devotee of "The Solomon School of Management," he instantly decided that the team would work nine-hour weekdays and half-day Saturdays. After the usual number of failed calls, Cecilia managed to inform each team member of her boss's decision. Naturally, it took a little extra explaining.

While her team sulked, Cecilia calculated the accumulated time it had taken to replace a one-hour meeting with person-to-person communications, as follows (in minutes):

Activity	Cecilia	Audit 1	Audit 2	Audit 3	Audit 4	Audit 5	Audit 6
Cecilia call failures	36	0	0	0	0	0	0
First calls to team	60	10	10	10	10	10	10
Team-to-team failures	0	10	10	10	10	10	10
Team connections	0	50	50	50	50	50	50
First report to Cecilia	60	10	10	10	10	10	10
Cecilia recall failures	36	0	0	0	0	0	0
Cecilia team recalls	60	10	10	10	10	10	10
Team-to-team failures	0	10	10	10	10	10	10
Second-call connections	0	50	50	50	50	50	50
Second report	60	10	10	10	10	10	10
The MP's decision	12	0	0	0	0	0	0
Cecilia re-recall failures	36	0	0	0	0	0	0
Cecilia team calls	90	15	15	15	15	15	15
Totals	450	175	175	175	175	175	175

Total time consumption was 1,500 minutes, or twenty-five person hours. A one-hour team meeting would have taken a total of seven person hours, so net lost productivity was eighteen hours. Moreover, each team member's work had been interrupted an average of seventeen times, a total of 102 disruptions versus seven for a comparable meeting. The decision was two days late. No one was happy with the final result.

The very next day, which was a Friday, Cecilia's team resumed its normal pattern of weekly get-togethers. Since then, the team has taken steps to improve meeting quality:

- An agenda is published at least one day before every meeting.
- Since a ten-minute delay caused by one thoughtless team member could result in seventy minutes of lost productivity and no small amount of irritation, every member of the team arrives on time.
- Every attendee sticks to the agenda.
- The meetings are concluded on time.

Once the pressure of the audit season was behind them, the managing partner asked Cecilia if she would like to repeat the test in order to confirm her results. Like any good boss who cared about the morale and productivity of her team, she graciously declined—on the spot.

Common Cause

*"In every age and clime we see
Two of a trade can never agree."*

—JOHN GAY

Since every company employee is on the same team, since there are so many futures at stake, and since there are so many barriers to be constantly overcome, it would seem that common cause would be common in business. It isn't.

A few years ago in Seattle, which is North America's only urban rain forest, a team of loggers was called in to fell a huge cedar tree that prevented the construction of a new software laboratory. Shortly thereafter, a bulldozer was brought in to remove the stump, but the stump was so large and so deeply entrenched that the bulldozer could not budge it. The foreman in charge of tree extraction circled the stump, carefully considered the problem, checked his watch, then called in three more bulldozers.

The new drivers, all of whom were independent contractors in competition with each other, individually surveyed the stump and the terrain upon arrival. Then each of the four bulldozer operators threw a chain around the stump, started up his bulldozer, threw it into low gear and commenced pulling.

On a hunch, the first bulldozer pulled toward the south. The second operator was convinced that he had a more powerful bulldozer than the first, so he pulled north. The third operator was certain that the stump was leaning toward the east, so he pulled in that direction. And the last operator was new to the profession and absolutely unwilling to work with any of the other three, so he pulled toward the west.

In the finest American tradition, each desperately wanted to defeat the others and succeed in pulling up the stump. So each operator pulled hard and each pulled long. Since each bulldozer had a two-hundred-horsepower engine, a large quantity of energy was expended in the effort. But the stump remained unmoved.

The foreman could see the problem. But he had started a small betting pool on the competition, and the loggers, big-shouldered men who did not like to be disappointed, had already placed their wagers. So rather than redirect the efforts of the bulldozers, the foreman doubled the quantity of gasoline and exhorted all four operators to try harder. Hours passed. Bulldozers strained against the load. Exhaust fumes filled the air. The foreman observed and exhorted. The loggers alternately cheered, booed, and did the wave. But still the stump was unmoved. Some time after darkness fell, they all reached a consensus to try again the following day.

The next morning, the CEO of the software company returned from an important business conference on the island of Bora Bora. Being a man in a hurry, he immediately increased the gasoline budget by a factor of five, he fired the operator with the most flagrant tattoos, he offered large bonuses to the three remaining operators if they succeeded in removing the stump by ten A.M., and he threatened to terminate everyone if the stump was not vanquished by lunchtime.

Leaving the foreman shaken but in control, the CEO sped off to an early tee time with an investment banker. He returned at noon to find the bulldozers inactive, the operators at lunch, the loggers on strike, the foreman in a deep depression, and the stump resolutely in place. Furious, the CEO fired the remaining operators and called in a professional negotiator to buy off the loggers. Then he hired a demolition expert to deal with the stump, he ordered the foreman to closely observe the execution of the new plan, and he hired an Ivy League consultant to explain the delay to the board of directors.

Fearing the fate of the foreman, the demolition expert used a large quantity of explosives. The stump, and its immediate environs, were vaporized.

After several months of careful study and a number of field tests, the consultant was able to conclude that only 250 horsepower would have been needed to extract the stump. A single bulldozer, which used an estimated 50 horsepower to impel itself through the mud, would have been able to apply a net force of only about 150 horsepower to the stump. But two bulldozers pulling in the same direction with an aggregate application of 300 horsepower would have easily removed the stump.

With a total of 600 net horsepower, four bulldozers should have been able to do the job easily. But the operators were more interested in competing than cooperating, so they all pulled in opposing directions. Thus, the net force applied to the stump was zero. The subsequent removal of the most artistic operator did not alter the result because two of the remaining three bulldozers continued to pull against each other. That caused the third to work alone against the stump, plus the mass and tension of the other two bulldozers.

Shortly after submitting his report to the board, the consultant was hired by the CEO to be the company's new chief financial officer. Some time later, three of the bulldozer operators decided to start a coffee company, although they have yet to agree on a name. Following an extensive recuperation period, the foreman retired to Arizona.

The CEO, who never learned the importance of common cause, was eventually elected to Congress after brief stints as an author and investment banker. It is not expected that his blind spot will hinder his new career.

Although it is rare in Congress (except during wartime, if then), common cause is how small companies defeat big companies. Two people who work together will always defeat four people, or six people or six hundred people, who find a reason to work against each other. But commitment to common cause is not just the acceptance of a single, common goal. Common cause also requires the subordination of personal agendas, which can be much more difficult.

Consensus at Work

"Consensus is the antidote for leadership."

—JULIAN DATE

Consensus is an agreement tool for family and business which, some believe, was originally perfected by the Japanese. Through team concurrence, its objectives are to minimize the likelihood of error and to ensure personal commitment to the execution of group decisions. In general, these are laudable intentions. But the tool cuts two ways and therefore must be used with care.

When he was a younger and truer man, Reginald DeNiall was the CEO of a software company called Cryptogram, which had created an encryption system for the secure electronic transmission of financial transactions between banks. Six years after start-up, the company had managed to achieve a significant share of the interbank market. In order to keep growing, however, Reginald and his management team knew that they would have to enter new markets.

Since he prided himself on being a modern business executive, Reginald assembled all seven members of his management team to brainstorm Cryptogram's next step. In a brief, six-hour meeting, they managed to determine that Cryptogram could expand into three new vertical markets: retail stores, telecommunications, or the defense industry. Alternatively, the company could remain in banking but expand horizontally into authentication systems, firewalls, or security-system integration.

These were too many possible directions for the company to take at one time. Choices had to be made. Accordingly, Reginald asked each of his six line managers to thoroughly research one of the potential new markets. The seventh "man," Cecilia Sharpe, who was Cryptogram's controller at the time, was asked to determine how many new directions the company could afford to pursue at once. Because there was so much to be done, and because they still had a company to run, the team agreed to reconvene four weeks later.

At the ensuing meeting, each of the six line managers presented the case for his market. Reginald was gratified to learn that each of the new markets had outstanding potential, but he was dismayed to observe that each of his line managers had come to prefer his own proposal. After six hours of presentation and three hours of debate, each manager still held to his original position.

Hoping for relief, Reginald turned to Cecilia. She informed him, however, that the company could afford to enter only one new market. Cecilia also knew that, presented with six equal options, the odds of consensus among the six line managers was approximately 1 in 8,000. (Unless suffering from a multiple personality disorder, one manager has a 100 percent probability of agreeing with himself. The odds of two managers agreeing on one of six equal choices is one in six, or 16.667 percent. Similarly, Reginald's probability of a consensus selection of one alternative among six by a group of six managers was equal to 16.667 percent to the fifth power, or approximately 00.013 percent.)

Clearly, some reduction in the number of alternatives was necessary. So Cecilia suggested to Reginald that each manager assist her in completing a detailed, five-year revenue and profit forecast for each market opportunity. After more discussion, everyone decided in favor of Cecilia's suggestion. Because there was so much to be done, and because they still had a company to run, they all agreed to get back together in one month.

The team reconvened on time, four weeks later. Each manager presented the business case for his market, including extensive financial forecasts that had been prepared by Cecilia. After a full day of presentations, discussion, and disappointment, the management team was able to reduce the number of potential choices to three:

- expansion into firewalls, which offered the highest long-term growth but which also had the highest up-front investment cost;
- authentication systems, which offered the highest long-term profit but which had the second-highest up-front cost; and
- expansion into the telecommunications market, which had the lowest up-front investment but which had only the fourth-ranked growth and profit forecast.

At that point, Reginald decided to take a straw poll of the entire management team. The results were not what any of them had hoped for: Three line managers favored the high-growth option; Reginald and another manager favored the high-profit option; Cecilia and the final two managers favored the low-investment option.

Frustrated, Reginald asked the team for suggestions on how to continue. Cecilia, who had already calculated the odds of eight managers' concurrence on one of three equal choices at about 1 in 2,200 (33.33 percent to the seventh power, or 00.046 percent), suggested that each manager rank the options in order of preference. Reginald, who was a career executive, instantly deduced that this would be a blatant circumvention of the consensus process. Lacking other viable suggestions but desperate to resolve the deadlock, he decided to bring in an expert from a major Boston consulting firm. Because the consultant would have so much to catch up on, and because the management team still had a company to run, they decided to get back together in a month.

Over the next four weeks, each member of the management team spent many hours with the outside consultant, who became well informed on each of the three remaining options. Each of Reginald's managers also had plenty of time to campaign for his personal preference.

To kick off the next meeting, Reginald asked the consultant to present his findings. After five hours of detailed review and no small amount of spirited discussion, Reginald took another straw poll. Option one was still preferred by the same three line managers; option two was preferred by Reginald, one line manager, and the consultant; Cecilia and the remaining two managers still preferred option three. Deadlock.

Once again, Cecilia suggested that each of them rank their preferences. The consultant, however, recommended a detailed, three-month study of the market. Knowing that the ninety-day period would be needed to construct the next year's budgets anyway, Reginald decided in favor of the consultant. Because there was so much to be done, they agreed not to reconvene until the consultant had finished his study and they had finished their budgets.

Four months later, everyone got back together except for one of the original managers, who had been replaced. The consultant presented his findings in detail. Then, after a full day of review, questions, and discussion, the consultant took a third straw poll. Reginald, the consultant, and three line managers, including the new addition, now favored option one while Cecilia and the remaining three line managers favored option three. Option two, unfortunately, had been eliminated due to recent market entry by a major competitor.

With only two alternatives remaining, Reginald turned to Cecilia. She knew, however, that the probability of 100 percent consensus on one of two equal choices among nine people was about 1 in 250. And, since ranking by order of preference would no longer be of value, she had no suggestions. The consultant, however, felt strongly that the only conscientious way of dealing with the deadlock was a detailed survey of future customer requirements.

Pleased that the company had not made a major mistake by choosing option two, Reginald concurred. Cecilia and the line managers in charge of marketing, sales, and customer service all agreed to assist with the study. Because there was so much to do, and because they still had a company to run, the team agreed to reconvene in three months.

Ninety days later, everyone met except the manager of marketing, who had resigned but had not been replaced. The consultant presented the findings of the customer survey in detail. After four hours of presentation and discussion, Reginald took another straw poll. Everyone now favored option one except Cecilia, who remained concerned that the high cost of a new software laboratory would put too much stress on the company's limited financial reserves. Sympathetic to her position, the consultant offered to study the possibility of outsourcing software development. At that exact moment, Cecilia's resistance collapsed. Reginald's consensus, which had been ten months in the making, was complete.

A few weeks later, Reginald invited his management team and the consultant to the local racetrack for some quality bonding time. By the third race, everyone had learned how to read the form and they were all placing their bets with fervor. Then, fifteen minutes before the post of the ninth and final race of the day, and possibly after a tad too much bonded refreshment, Cecilia suggested that they all bet their next paycheck on the same horse, and only to win.

MB(U)O

"The bow too tensely strung is easily broken."

—PUBLIUS SYRUS

Businesses almost always perform better when each employee in the business knows what his or her objectives are. That is why a technique called Management by Objective, or MBO, was invented. Unfortunately, MBO may not be the most commonly practiced form of the discipline in some companies, which may explain, with the assistance of Reginald DeNiall, the insertion of the *U* in MBUO.

After Cryptogram's management team had so much difficulty in reaching a consensus on market expansion, Reginald DeNiall had no choice but to convince the board of directors to accept a revenue growth objective of just 33 percent for the succeeding financial year. Being a firm believer in Management by Objective, Reginald began the process of parceling out the annual goal to his management team within days of the conclusion of the board meeting.

Most of the goal-setting process was not difficult. The exception was sales. Since the consensus had taken so long, there would be no revenue from the new market in the coming year. But the diversification would absorb virtually all of the company's investment capacity, so the existing sales force would have to shoulder the burden of company growth.

Reginald believed that his sales force had the capability. However, like many executives, he worried that the best of them would not close all of the sales they were capable of closing. Called "putting the order in the drawer," it was a common practice, especially among sales representatives who made quota well before the end of the year. Given a 33 percent revenue growth target in a slow growth market, Reginald knew that he could not afford to have any business postponed into the future. So Reginald decided to increase the sales quota slightly, by only 12.5 percent, which made the target a total of $54 million, an $18 million increase over the previous year's business.

The vice president of sales was intimately aware of the conditions in Cryptogram's existing market. But he also knew that arguing with the $54 million objective could be construed as a sign of weakness. So instead of debating the point, he focused on figuring out how to distribute the revenue objective among his sales managers.

On the surface, it appeared that each of the six sales managers would be required to shoulder a new year revenue objective of $9 million. But the vice president was worried that only three or four of them would be able to reach the goal and that the failure of the others would drag down the overall performance of his group. To make sure that his best performers performed at their best, he decided to increase the revenue target for his sales managers slightly, to an average of $10 million each.

The six sales managers, who had produced an average of $6 million in sales revenue the current year, were not enthused by the 67 percent growth in their quotas. Given the conditions of the market, it was not at all clear that the average representative could increase sales by so much in the coming year. Obviously, some stars would be needed to lift the overall performance of each sales team. So the sales managers conferred with each other and decided to raise individual sales quotas slightly, from an average of $1.67 million to an average of $2 million.

Thus, by the time that new year's revenue target reached the field, it had increased from the CEO's objective of $48 million, or $1.33 million per sales representative, to an average of $2 million per salesman and a total sales target of $72 million.

Over the course of the ensuing year, the sales team worked very hard. Eight of the thirty-six sales representatives actually made quota, producing an average of $2.5 million in sales revenue each. Sixteen representatives, however, failed to reach the target, producing an average of just $1.5 million, or just 75 percent of quota for the year. The other twelve sales representatives left the company before the year's end. Although new salesmen were hired, they had to restart activity in their respective territories after being trained. As a result, the twelve territories affected by attrition produced just $8 million in revenue for the year, only $667,000 per territory and less than 34 percent of objective.

So, overall, Cryptogram produced $52 million in sales revenue, 8.33 percent above the Board's target for a "tough" year and 44 percent above the previous year's performance. The sales vice president, however, finished the year $2 million below his quota of $54 million. As a result, he was excluded from the spring sales trip, he was chastised for unplanned attrition within his organization, and he got no raise in salary.

The six sales managers produced an average of $8.67 million in revenue, up 44.5 percent from the previous year's average of $6 million. But four of the six failed to make their $10 million quotas and two of them were subsequently terminated.

Eleven of the sixteen sales representatives who finished the year but who failed to reach their $2 million quotas eventually left the company, continuing the decimation of the sales force into a second year. Even so, they had increased their personal productivity by an average of 50 percent, from $1 million to $1.5 million, which was better than the company as a whole.

Nevertheless, it was a very successful year for Reginald, who, despite a downturn in profits due to heavy end-of-year discounting, got a raise, a one-year contract extension, and more stock options. In the following spring, which turned out to be his last as CEO at Cryptogram, he took his eight star sales representatives and two star sales managers on a business trip to the South Pacific.

Management by Objective can be a good thing. Certainly it is far better for employees to know their objectives than to guess at them. But if the original objectives are stretched at each layer of management, even slightly, then they will compound. It is an arithmetic certainty. Thus, MBO at the board level can quickly escalate into MBUO, which means Management by Unobtainable Objective, by the time it reaches the bottom rung of the company where actual work is done.

Cryptogram's management team had an alternative. Instead of being seduced by MBUO, they could have increased the average quota of its sales force to $1.33 million and hired six to nine new representatives in anticipation of attrition and expected growth. As a result, objectives would have been equalized up and down the organization and everyone, regardless of level, would have had the same chance to succeed or fail—together.

CHAPTER

19

The Mystery of Middle Management

"Man is by nature a political animal."

—ARISTOTLE

Managers have been with us since the beginning of history. It is well documented, for instance, that managers were involved in the construction of the Great Pyramids of Egypt. And the Greeks invented education managers, whom we call teachers, although no one knows who invented principals. But even before the Egyptians or the Greeks, there were chieftains in virtually every known tribe. And long before that ancient time, there were cave managers, commonly called parents, who formed an institution so resilient and successful that it survives today in some of the planet's more primitive regions.

In the postmodern age of information, management has become a science, just like everything else. Its most advanced forms, like MB(U)O, are most often encountered in business. But ironically, the most complex management challenge of contemporary times may be the executive branch of the U.S. government. This is a single, cohesive organization of some 2,800,000 employees, all of whom work for the president of the United States under the watchful eye of freshman Congressman Reginald DeNiall and his colleagues.

A lot of those 2.8 million federal employees are managers, perhaps too many. And managers, by definition, do not do real work, especially middle managers. So, what if, with the exception of the president, all of the management positions in the executive branch were eliminated?

As enticing as this may seem, especially from a cost saving point of view, there might be a few complications. Most important, the president would have to communicate government policy directly to each and every one of his 2.8 million federal employees. (This is the humane management elimination model, wherein all managers are given real jobs rather than being terminated—which, no doubt, the affected managers would also do if faced with a similar challenge.) In the perspective of an average, fifty-six-hour workweek, the simple task of communicating to each employee turns out to be a daunting challenge, even for a very succinct president. And, arguably, a succinct president may never have been elected in the entirety of American history.

Nevertheless, if a recently managementless but uniquely succinct president undertook to speak to the entire employee population of the executive branch in groups of ten every month, and if the president devoted fifty-six hours per week (and four weeks per month) to this important task, then he (or she, someday, presumably) would be able to devote approximately 2.9 seconds to each meeting, exclusive of preparation and travel time. It is not likely that

2.9 seconds per month would be adequate time for the full communication and discussion of federal policy, much less day-to-day workload. Over the course of a full four-year term, the president would be able to spend only about two minutes and eighteen seconds with any group of employees, certainly an insufficient amount of time for discussion, bonding, or the establishment of camaraderie.

If the average group were increased to one thousand federal employees, which would probably eliminate any opportunity for bonding or camaraderie with the president, then the average monthly get-together could last almost five minutes. However, if 50 percent of each meeting were devoted to questions and answers, and if the answers were no longer than the questions, then each employee would have just .07 seconds to ask a question. Worse, the president would have just .07 seconds per answer, which would limit most presidents to a paragraph or two.

Luckily, our government does not suffer from such a self-imposed dearth of management. In fact, the president is required by law to appoint the more senior of them after election. These appointments are the most important positions in government: secretaries, undersecretaries, agency directors, commissioners, and ambassadors. So the task of selecting the best person for the best job must be taken very seriously.

For a similarly critical job in business, it might be expected that the chief executive would spend at least an hour with five candidates for each position, another hour with each of two finalists, and one hour cementing the relationship with the surviving applicant. (In comparison, every Intel interviewee, regardless of position, is required to undergo at least five interviews.)

However, according to the Office of Personnel Management, each newly elected United States president must make 2,899 such appointments, more than 110 of which report directly to the Oval Office. Assuming a fifty-six-hour work-week and eight hours of interviews per position, the president would be able to appoint only seven new government executives each week. At that rate, assuming no vacation time, it would take the president a little more than 414 weeks to fill all of the appointed jobs in the executive branch. Four hundred and fourteen weeks is just two weeks short of two full presidential terms. This would mean that 99.6 percent of government business would be left unmanaged for eight years, which may explain one of the more popular theories in the general electorate.

Of course, the president does have a few things to do other than interview federal management aspirants, one of which is getting himself reelected. So, obviously, some hiring shortcuts have to be found. If, however, the president commits to completing all of the necessary appointments in the first six months of his term, and if he can devote an average of sixteen hours per week to this critical task, then he can afford to spend an average of just under nine minutes per appointment. This is probably insufficient, even for the heads of the Panama Canal Commission and the Marine Mammal Commission, both of whom report directly to the Oval Office. And nine minutes is almost certainly an inadequate amount of time to qualify even a single political candidate to direct the Office of Government Ethics.

There is no commercial enterprise of any kind that imposes such a burden on its chief executive. In fact, most modern corporations tend to operate with an average span of control (the number of direct reports to each manager) of between eight to one and twelve to one. If the executive branch of government were organized along the lines of a similar model, perhaps a span of control of eight or nine to one, then the president's job would be dramatically simplified, as follows:

Management Level	Number of Employees	Cumulative Employees
President	1	1
VP and Secretaries	9	10
Undersecretaries (9:1)	81	91
Commissioners (8:1)	648	739
Directors (8:1)	5,184	5,923
Managers (8:1)	41,472	47,395
Supervisors (8:1)	331,776	379,171
Actual Workers (8:1)	2,654,208	3,033,379

This structure seems to create a lot of middle managers. But the advantages are:

1. No employee is more than six persons removed from the Oval Office.
2. The president is directly responsible for only eight appointments, the rest could be delegated to the vice president and the secretaries.
3. The president has much more time to focus on meetings with key direct and indirect reports, especially during times of crisis.
4. The president has more time to spend in intimate, win/win brainstorming sessions with representatives of the House and Senate.
5. The size of the White House staff could be dramatically

reduced (the executive branch was originally intended to be the president's staff).

6. Even after reorganization, less than 13 percent of the federal government would be middle managers (directors, managers, and supervisors).

In addition, the election of a Washington outsider would be less likely to become an overnight, full-employment program for the president-elect's hometown.

Of course, presiding over the federal government and managing a business are not the same. No private sector CEO, for instance, has to deal with a Congress, approximately half of whom are habitually hostile to the aspirations of the president at any given time.

Maybe that's why we have come to expect so much from our elected officials.

Calculating Behavior

*"None of us really understands what's
going on with all these numbers."*

—DAVID STOCKMAN (ON THE 1981 FEDERAL BUDGET)

Figures Don't Lie ...

*"Mathematics may be defined as the subject
in which we never know what we are talking about,
nor whether what we are saying is true."*

—BERTRAND RUSSELL

J ust like cereal and cigarettes, numbers are packaged for the convenience of the consumer audience. But there are few truth-in-labeling laws for numbers, so the czars of marketing have plenty of room for creativity.

A few years ago, and shortly after a costly and embarrassing confrontation with an entrenched tree stump, Reginald DeNiall decided to sell his software company. Given the company's rapid growth during his administration, he was confident that he could get a very good price, especially within the high-technology industry. So, like all good CEOs, Reginald set about preparing his organization for sale. First, he divorced his wife, who was also his controller, and replaced her in the company with a high-powered chief financial officer (called a CFO in the trade) who had recently been a consultant with an important eastern firm.

Reginald and the new CFO then drafted a prospectus, which is a lot like a brochure, only it is specifically for the sale of a company. The cover letter of the prospectus did an excellent job of extolling the virtues of the company's performance over the previous four years, which included:

- three consecutive years of profitability;
- average growth of 35 percent in the previous four years; and
- a 9 percent reduction in expenses in the last twelve months.

A dozen major software companies and independent investors examined Reginald's company closely. However, despite the excellent prospectus, the upgraded management team, and the obvious benefits of Reginald's focus on company growth, they all declined the acquisition. A contributing factor was the company's actual financial performance during Reginald's presidency, which was as follows (in millions of dollars):

	Year 1	Year 2	Year 3	Year 4
Revenue	$22.4	$36.0	$52.0	$45.4
Expenses	$19.1	$33.1	$51.5	$46.9
Pretax Profits	$3.3	$2.9	$.5	−$1.5

Although everything that Reginald claimed in the prospectus was true, the company's actual financial performance had been somewhat different:

- Profits had declined for three consecutive years, from a very respectable 14.7 percent of revenues in Reginald's first year as CEO to a 3.3 percent loss in his final year;

- Growth, which had averaged more than 50 percent in the previous two years, had reversed to a 13 percent decline in the last twelve months; and
- Expenses were dropping, but they were dropping more slowly than revenues, leading potential investors to predict even greater losses in the years ahead.

Being a man of conviction, Reginald eventually sold the company to a Swiss confectioner at a price much lower than he'd hoped, then wrote a book and subsequently joined the investment banking firm that had helped him to complete the sale. Shortly thereafter, with the support of both his new employer and his political party, Reginald managed to place himself on the ballot for a congressional seat that had recently become vacant due to the usual sex scandal.

Reginald's opponent in the primary was a clean-cut health nut, which would not have mattered much except that Reginald, who reads for exercise, is from a state in the Pacific Northwest that is chock-full of health nuts who vote.

As the primary neared, the opponent moved ahead of Reginald in the polls, thanks to a simple television campaign in which he jogged down a typical neighborhood street, dressed in a patriotic, blue and green "Go Mariners" sweat suit, while he emphasized his fitness for the job of congressman. Everywhere Reginald looked, he saw his opponent on a billboard in a jogging suit. Every time he turned on the television, Reginald saw his opponent running on at the mouth about fitness for Congress.

Reginald, who had come to believe that integrity was a

communications tool, did not see how he could possibly lose to an anonymous, kid liberal whose principal virtue was exercise. But as election day neared and the gap widened to three percentage points in the polls, Reginald became more and more depressed.

Then, on a dark and dreary night about two weeks before the primary, Reginald happened to be watching the eleven o'clock news on KWET, an independent television station north of Seattle. The headline story, and the first ten minutes of the broadcast, were solely devoted to the plight of the state's recently elected governor. It featured an in-depth studio report, a broadcast from the governor's mansion, a historical perspective, several "expert interviews," and an "on the scene" update from a picturesque Colorado hospital—all to report that the new governor had fractured his arm in a skiing accident.

Reginald's mood was transformed by the media's enthusiasm for the governor's minor mishap. He picked up the telephone and called his campaign manager, who had formerly been his CFO. That same night, after thoroughly analyzing the situation, the two of them concluded that Reginald could still win the primary if they could find a way to defeat the core virtue of his rival's campaign: his fitness ethic.

The campaign manager immediately launched an in-depth investigation of his opponent's habits. In the meantime, Reginald's media director prepared the press for the possibility of a small but significant scandal. Then, two days before the election, Reginald's team leaked its findings to an animated and eager media community.

One day before the election:

- The local television news reported that the candidate's exercise routine was a model of inconsistency in which he exercised twice in three days, then once in the next four.
- A cable network talk show reported that Reginald's opponent, who claimed to be a fitness fanatic, actually exercised less than 3 percent of the time.
- An editorial in the state's most influential newspaper reported that Reginald's opponent went three days per week without exercising at all.
- A radio network reported that he often exercised only once in five days.

Reginald, of course, was dismayed to learn that his opponent, who was so prideful of his fitness focus, could have such a lightweight exercise routine. In the hours leading up to the primary, he managed to convey the message many times in a statewide media blitz.

In his concession speech immediately following the election, Reginald's opponent detailed his exercise regimen to the press. It turned out that he completed a rigorous, ninety-minute routine that included calisthenics, free weights, and a two-mile run, between six and seven-thirty A.M. every Monday, Wednesday, and Friday.

A junior reporter for a suburban newspaper later figured out that all three exercise routines were actually completed in an elapsed time of 97.5 hours (four days plus 1.5 hours). That meant that the losing candidate did not exercise at all for 70.5 hours, which is 2.9375 days and which rounds easily to three. In addition, two of the three routines were completed in only 49.5 hours, which meant that there was only one routine in the next 118.5 hours, which was 4.9375 days. Unfortunately, the newspaper's editor did not elect to publish the reporter's findings since it was not at all clear that the article would maximize the wealth of the parent company's shareholders by increasing circulation.

Reginald had his agendas. So do the media, business, and charity. Always exercise caution when dealing with any numbers that they package for your consumption. Better yet, take a few moments to add them up for yourself.

The Duke of Pork

"A billion here, a billion there, and pretty soon you're talking about real money."

—EVERETT DIRKSEN

Light travels at about 186,282 miles per second, so it should have taken about 0.015 seconds for news of Reginald DeNiall's election to the House of Representatives to travel 2,788 miles from Seattle to the nation's capital. Somehow, though, it seemed like the news got there even faster than that, possibly because of the sincere admiration so many of Reginald's new peers had for the creative way in which he had managed the final days of his campaign.

This admiration became a matter of serendipity a few weeks later when Reginald was invited to dinner at the Washington, D.C., home of one of the most powerful men in Congress, who was nicknamed the "Gentleman from the South." That evening, over fried chicken, corn bread, sweet potatoes, black-eyed peas, and homemade biscuits, the Gentleman offered Reginald the opportunity to represent his party on the powerful House Ways and Means Committee.

This was an unexpected honor for a rookie congressman. The honor had a price. It was that Reginald would vigorously support his host's campaign for reelection some eighteen months hence.

Reginald, who had generally taken to Capitol politics like a young vulture takes to fresh carrion, intuitively understood what his new benefactor wanted. It wasn't votes, which hadn't won an election of consequence since 1960. It was leverage in his district, which meant money. Reginald guessed that his host wanted a lot of it, so he asked how much. Over bread pudding with vanilla sauce, he was answered with a quotation attributed to the late Senator Dirksen of Illinois.

For a lesser man, this might have seemed an impossible task. The Gentleman's home state was not particularly wealthy, and he had less than a 25 percent approval rating in the rest of the United States, so large, "indirect" campaign contributions were out of the question. Reginald, however, was a businessman who believed in the power of capitalism, so he did his homework, or rather his staff did. A few weeks later, Reginald proposed a business solution to the problem, one that was faithfully implemented by the Gentleman from the South shortly thereafter.

In the very next federal budget, which was passed by his party's majority in both the House and the Senate, a major aerospace manufacturer in the Gentleman's home state received an unexpected appropriation for $1 billion in military transport aircraft. No other company could build those airplanes, so jobs were created, property prices were increased, and businessmen were enriched. In addition, since procurement of those same aircraft had not been requested by the U.S. Air Force in nearly a decade, there was no question about who was really responsible for both the budget line item and the contract award.

Better yet, the cost of the airplanes was not borne solely by taxpayers in the Congressman's district. Instead, it was shared equally by 139 million taxpayers across the country. Therefore, even though only one in four voters approved of the Gentleman from Georgia outside of his home state, each and every American taxpayer was required to contribute more than seven dollars to his next campaign for reelection.

Since those aircraft will remain in service for many more years, it can be expected that the long-term cost of parts and maintenance will eclipse the original manufacturing price. This means that the American people will eventually be taxed more than two billion dollars, which is a tax assessment of more than $14 per taxpayer, to preserve the congressman's position, which paid approximately $136,600 per annum (at the time).

Since two billion dollars is more than 14,000 times larger than $136,000, paying that much to preserve a single congressman's job might not seem entirely sensible. But, to an up-and-coming political entrepreneur like Reginald DeNiall, the capital's newly crowned "Duke of Pork," it smelled of opportunity.

Maybe Reginald is on to something. If the deficit is not a concern, as so many Congressmen selflessly contend, then perhaps we should consider extending the principles of pork to the entirety of Congress. Since senators only run for reelection every sixth year, we could subsidize their re-election campaigns to the tune of a billion dollars each at an annualized cost of only $16.7 billion or so.

There are 435 Representatives in the House and they run for reelection every two years. Therefore, the annualized cost of extending "The Reginald Plan" to them would be around $217.5 billion. The total congressional pork tab would add up to just $234.2 billion dollars per year, or about $1,685 dollars per taxpayer per year.

Of course, besides being somewhat costly when extended to the fullness of Congress, that one billion dollar reelection subsidy could provide each incumbent with an overwhelming advantage. Certainly, it would be impossible for all but a handful of very rich challengers to raise even a tenth of that in campaign contributions. Thus, the continued existence of pork barrel spending, even for an influential few, may eloquently explain why the president of the United States does not have the line item veto and, in some part, why the U.S. government carries the largest debt ever known to mankind.

22

The National Debt

*"Politics is the distance between
what makes sense and what gets done."*

—JULIAN DATE

As of mid-1998, the United States, which means us, had a national debt of about 5.54 trillion dollars. In real numbers that is $5,540,000,000,000. Most folks, maybe even a congressman or two, believe that to be a fairly large sum of money.

The 5.54 trillion-dollar national debt is how much money the U.S. government has had to borrow over the years because it has spent more than it has collected in taxes. The U.S. government borrows money by selling bonds—mostly treasury bonds, treasury bills, and savings bonds—to anyone who will buy them (foreign investors own about 25 percent). In return for lending Uncle Sam the money, the bondholders are entitled to receive interest on the loan.

In 1997, the interest on the national debt was about

$356,000,000,000. That means the U.S. government paid more for interest on its outstanding loans than it paid for defense, or education, or welfare, or medicare, or anything else.

Of course, the U.S. government doesn't really pay the interest on the national debt. U.S. taxpayers pay it. In 1997, the interest bill alone was more than $2,500 for each and every taxpaying citizen. That is almost $50 per taxpayer per week, just for interest on the federal government's accumulated debt.

Unfortunately, it wasn't enough. For the twenty-ninth consecutive year, the U.S. government did not take in enough in taxes to conduct its affairs and pay all of that interest. So again in 1997, the U.S. government had to borrow more money. That is called the deficit. According to the U.S. Bureau of Public Debt, the deficit was only $188 billion in 1997, the lowest figure in many years. (From September 1989 through September 1992, the last Republican administration before President Clinton, the national debt climbed from $2.86 trillion to $4.41 trillion, an average annual deficit of more than $388 billion per year.)

Luckily, the Democrats and the Republicans managed to balance the budget in 1998—or, more accurately, they allowed the strength of the economy to balance the budget without congressional interference. Lest you get too excited, this only means that the annual deficit was eliminated for one consecutive year (although 1999 also looks promising).

However, balancing the budget does not mean that the national debt has been paid back. It's still there. It's just not getting bigger anymore. But if the national debt is never paid back, then the interest on the debt will have to be paid forever. Even for sea turtles, forever is a fairly long time. In fact, unless the U.S. government can find a way to spend less money than it takes in, which means an annual budget surplus, then the interest bill on the national debt will be infinitely large.

For instance, if the national debt stabilizes at 5.5 trillion dollars and the government can continue to borrow money at a steady 6 percent interest, then the interest on the national debt will average around $330,000,000,000 per year. Over the next fifty years, that is a total interest bill of $16.5 trillion, three times the size of the national debt itself. Yet the national debt will remain at a steady $5.5 trillion.

If the national debt remains flat, however, then the amount of money each citizen will have to pay each year will go down. That is because the U.S. population is growing— at a rate of about one person every sixteen seconds (one birth every eight seconds, one death every thirteen seconds, one new immigrant every forty-three seconds, plus adjustments for migration). That is a net increase in population of about 5,400 people per day, or just under two million per year. The U.S. Census Bureau estimates, in fact, that U.S. population will reach 322 million by the year 2020. If the national debt is still $5,540,000,000,000, then the average citizen's debt load will be about $17,200, a 16 percent improvement over the $20,500 or so that each citizen owes today.

Inflation will also help. At an average of 5 percent inflation, the value of a 1999 dollar will drop to about 34 cents in the year 2020. So the discounted value of each citizen's national debt load could be as low as $5,850, a whopping 71 percent improvement over the current situation.

That, in fact, appears to be The Plan. On paper it looks

workable. But more things can go wrong. If the national debt increases to ten trillion dollars by the year 2020, which is less than 3 percent annual growth, the average annual interest rate increases to only 8 percent, then the government's yearly interest bill will jump to about $800,000,000,000. For those of you who find that worrisome, that is only about $2.2 billion per day, including weekends. If it happens, then the nation's 161 million taxpaying citizens will have to pay an average of $4,969 in interest alone that year, which is more than $95 per taxpayer per week (compared to a cost of around $50 per taxpayer per week in 1997).

In fact, the national debt is already so large that it will not be paid off in the lifetime of any taxpayer reading this book. This means that we will all be paying interest on it every day for the rest of our taxpaying lives. All of us. The only question is whether the same will be true for our grandchildren, their children, and their children.

Cecilia Sharpe does not expect to be able to retire until the year 2020. Between now and then, she expects to pay about twice as much tax as the U.S. average. Even if the national debt remains level at $5.54 trillion dollars until then, and even if the taxpayer base grows to 161 million, then Cecilia is forecast to pay more than $100,000 in interest on the national debt before she retires. By herself.

If the deficit returns to a growth rate of just 3 percent of the national debt per year, then the national debt will grow to more than $10 billion by the year 2020. Between now and then, Cecilia will have to pay more than $137,500 in interest on the national debt. In the year 2020 alone, she will pay more than $7,600. By herself.

However, if the national debt is reduced by a mere 3 percent per year starting in the year 2000, then it will drop to a relatively paltry $2.92 trillion by the year 2020. Between now and then, Cecilia will still pay almost $75,000 in interest. But the last year's bill is forecast to be less than $2,200, reflecting a much better future for her daughter Gwendolyn.

The forecast differences are worth summarizing:

Change in national debt per year	National debt in 2020	Cecilia's 21-year interest bill	Cecilia's last interest bill
+3%	$10.30 trillion	$137,500	$7,680
Flat	$5.54 trillion	$100,000	$4,130
3%	$2.92 trillion	$74,800	$2,200

In order for the third case to have a chance, Congress must stop spending billions of dollars to preserve a few jobs. More important, it must stop cutting taxes every two to four years in an attempt to buy everybody's reelection. That is because taxes can be "cut" only when the budget is in surplus. When there is a deficit, then every "tax cut" is a tax postponement. Taxpayers don't pay for the postponed taxes immediately, but the tax shortfalls accumulate in the national debt. In turn, we pay more interest on the debt—which goes on and on and on and on and on.

In other words, every "tax cut" in the twentieth century has really been a veiled tax increase. The accumulated cost of all of these generous "tax cuts" is trillions of dollars of past and future interest on the national debt.

We have left our children and grandchildren a legacy of

debt—the largest and most irresponsible debt in the history of mankind. Our only hope of forgiveness is to start repaying it. It means that, except in times of war or prolonged recession, the U.S. government must run an annual surplus every year until the debt is repaid.

Debts are not monuments. They should not last forever. They should be repaid. If, however, loans are allowed to exist in perpetuity, then so will the interest on them, which means that the cost of borrowing will be infinitely high.

The national debt is colossal, but it must not be turned into a monument. It can and should be paid in full. Until then, any new "tax cut" is really a tax increase. Until the national debt is history, there are two legitimate ways to cut taxes: reduce the cost of government or increase taxes. Until the national debt is repaid, there are no other responsible courses of action.

Even if we start to repay the national debt today, we will leave trillions of dollars in debt to future generations. This is money we spent on ourselves but which future generations never agreed to lend us. In fact, they were never even asked. That is called taxation without representation. Our founding fathers thought it was wrong. We should, too.

23

Personal Debt

"Let us all be happy to live within our means,
even if we have to borrow the money to do it with."

—CHARLES FARRAR BROWNE

Loan companies advertise a lot on television these days, but they don't sell credit. They sell privilege: the freedom to go anywhere, the money to buy anything, special discounts, and, of course, status.

Americans are willing to pay big for privilege, freedom, and status. There are more than 30,000 different credit cards available in the United States; the average American adult carries six of them. In 1996, we Americans paid an average of $3,900 per person in interest on credit card and installment debt. Our total debts added up to 95 percent of our income. We must have a lot of privilege and status.

In truth, the credit card companies, the bankers, and the mortgage lenders are not selling freedom or privilege or status. They are selling money. Since they are in the business of selling money, they expect to get more back than they originally sold. The difference between how much they sell and how much they get back is called interest.

The borrower is the buyer. In order to get the money, the borrower signs a contract agreeing to pay the lender more, sometimes a lot more, than the amount borrowed. Except for credit cards, which have a very high interest rate, there is usually some form of security. Failure to repay an automobile loan, for example, will normally result in the loss of the vehicle along with a number of other unhappy consequences.

Reginald DeNiall, who enjoys an excellent credit rating, recently bought his youngest son, Billy Ray, a new Dodge pickup truck after he agreed to finish high school. Since Reginald is a congressman, he got a special deal on the loan. He borrowed 100 percent of the truck's heavily discounted $20,000 price tag, to be repaid over four years at 10 percent interest compounded monthly. Over the full term of the loan, Reginald will pay more than $4,400 in interest on the pickup, or about 22 percent of the original purchase price. Billy Ray believes that this is a small price to pay for freedom and status. Reginald, of course, is actually paying the bill.

Regardless of what most of us may think about the high cost of borrowing, almost all of us have to borrow money in order to buy a house or a condominium. These days, the typical loan is for more than $100,000 and the term is 15 to 30 years. Over such a long period of time, the cost of the interest is so high that the mortgage lender ends up getting more money than the builder of the house.

But there are two important differences to consider. First, the U.S. government allows its citizens to deduct mortgage interest from taxable income, which significantly reduces the cost of the loan. Second, houses tend to appreciate in value. So they can frequently (although not always) be sold for more than the purchase price. As a result, buying a home is generally (but not always) better than renting. However, if the house payment is too high, it can choke the cash flow out of anyone. And the fees for buying and selling a home are expensive, usually 5 percent to 7 percent of the purchase price. So most homes must be owned for quite a few years before a profit can be made on their sale.

Although Reginald's elder son, Joe Bob DeNiall, has an excellent manufacturing job with a respected local firm, he can't afford a condo yet. But he does have two major credit cards of his very own. As soon as he got the first one, he went right out and used it to get a $2,000 stereo. The interest on the credit card is 18 percent, or 1.5 percent per month. So Joe Bob has to pay the bank $30 per month in interest for the right to continue to use the stereo. But even though Joe Bob pays each monthly bill on time, the balance he owes on his credit cards keeps going up because he keeps charging more. Last month, he "bought" a new game system for his TV set—which he had charged the month before that.

If Joe Bob has a $5,000 credit limit on his two credit cards (his father is a congressman), and if he keeps them at the maximum balance for ten years, then he will pay a total of $9,000 in interest, almost twice as much as he originally borrowed. Moreover, he will have to earn $12,000 to $14,000 so he will have enough money after taxes to pay the $9,000 in interest. And he will still owe $5,000.

To young folks in particular, that first credit card is as precious as a puppy: It is cute and cuddly; it cries for attention; it must be exercised frequently; and it's fun to show off. Puppies, however, grow into dogs. If your loan portfolio has matured into Lassie, then your debt is your pal. But, if your cumulative interest load has grown into an 800-pound pit bull that consumes its own weight in cash every thirty days, you have a serious financial problem. You may need professional help.

It is more likely, though, that you can work your way out of debt's doghouse. Start by replacing all of those credit cards with a debit card, which is less dangerous by nature. Otherwise, use cash. Or write a check. Or take a bath. Because, if you have to charge it, you can't really afford it.

24

Investing Young

*"Wealth has its advantages, and the case
to the contrary, although often made,
has never proved widely persuasive."*

—JOHN KENNETH GALBRAITH

All but a lucky few have to save for retirement. Since the "golden years" are so far in the distance, many young people postpone this important activity until middle age. However, how much money you accumulate by retirement will depend upon three things: when you start saving, how much you manage to save each year, and how much your investments return over the long run. Of the three, when you start saving turns out to be the most important.

Cecilia Sharpe, who has a reputation for good financial sense throughout the community, began putting $2,000 in an IRA-approved mutual fund, which returns 7 percent per year, when she was only twenty-five years old. When she is sixty-five years old, that first year's $2,000 investment will be worth almost $29,400 all by itself.

Feeling mortal on his forty-fifth birthday, Reginald

DeNiall decided to open an IRA and invest the same amount in the same mutual fund. Unfortunately, at age sixty-five, his $2,000 investment will be worth only a little more than $7,700.

Both invested exactly $2,000. They will each get exactly the same return per year. The length of Reginald's investment will be exactly half as long as Cecilia's. But the amount Reginald will have at retirement will be only 26 percent as much.

That's because interest compounds. Compounding means that interest is paid not only on the original $2,000 investment each year but also on all of the interest that has accumulated over previous years. At 7 percent interest, for instance, $140 is added to Cecilia's $2,000 investment at the end of the first year. But at the end of the second year, $149.80 is added—$140 for the original investment and $9.80 for the previous year's $140 interest. This never seems like much in the beginning, so saving is easy to put off. But compounding pays off in the long run—because the amount of interest eventually exceeds the amount of the original investment. Over the very long run, in fact, accumulated interest dwarfs investment.

Consistency is just as critical as starting young. Cecilia has invested $2,000 in her 7 percent IRA every year so far and plans to continue investing the same amount every year until retirement. After forty years, her $80,000 investment will be worth more than $419,000.

Unwilling to face a retirement lifestyle inferior to Cecilia's despite his twenty-year handicap, Reginald decided to invest $6,000 every year, three times as much as Cecilia. However, the CPA on his research staff quickly informed the congressman that he would still have only $263,000 in his IRA at retirement (even if he could really afford to set aside as much as $6,000 per year, which was $4,000 more than he had managed to put into an IRA in any previous year).

This was a sad state of affairs. Those who knew Reginald's competitive spirit feared that he would eventually resort to speculation on stock options, commodities, and low-grade bonds. The returns on such investments can be beguiling, sometimes as much as 30 percent or more. But because of their volatile nature, the high returns are often diluted by large losses.

Through his experience with Social Security legislation, however, Reginald was certain that he could catch up to Cecilia, no matter how late he started. As a member of Congress, Reginald also believed that he had a special insight into how certain segments of the economy would perform in the near-to-intermediate term. And he had the advantage of an excellent research staff.

Once again, therefore, Reginald decided to amend his investment strategy by keeping his annual IRA contribution at a less painful $2,000 but investing it in high-risk stock and bond funds. In the ensuing two years, his IRA returned 30 percent per year on an annual investment of $2,000. In the third year, he lost 30 percent.

Compared to Cecilia, whose IRA continued to return an uninspiring 7 percent each and every year, Reginald's three-year return was as follows:

	Reginald	Cecilia	Difference
Value at End of Year 1	$2,600	$2,140	$460
Value at End of Year 2	$3,380	$2,289	$1091
Value at End of Year 3	$2,366	$2,450	-$84

Reginald was irate. He could not understand how he could make 30 percent per year in two out of three years but still underperform a paltry 7 percent per year. After all, three years at 7 percent was a total of only 21 percent, but his return over the same period had been 30 percent (30 percent in each of the first two years, less 30 percent in the third).

Reginald's accountant replied that a 30 percent return in two or three years, although a very high return and a success rate of 67 percent, would always underperform a consistent return of only 7 percent per year, as follows:

- Three years at a consistent +7 percent interest —> 1.07 x 1.07 x 1.07 = 1.225
- Three years @ +30 percent, +30 percent, -30 percent—> 1.3 x 1.3 x .7 = 1.183

In fact, because of the single year loss, the last two years of Reginald's investment strategy had produced a total return of -9 percent. That is because 130 percent times 70 percent is not 100 percent; it is only 91 percent. The accountant then made Reginald a chart that showed how much an investment of $2,000 would be worth in the long run, assuming that a 67 percent speculative success rate was sustainable:

Long-Term Return

Investment Length	7%/yr.	+30%/+30%/-30%
12 Years	$4,504	$3.917
24 Years	$10,144	$7,672
36 Years	$22,848	$15,026

Finally, the accountant suggested to Reginald that he simply invest in stocks, which, according to all the advertisements, had averaged a 10 percent return over the very long run and which, therefore, would produce a sum of $19,700 in only 24 years for each $2,000 invested. Frustrated with his inability to sustain high rates of return, Reginald was more than happy to agree.

The accountant, who must have been distracted by the preparation of his résumé at the time, unfortunately forgot to tell Reginald that most stock return calculations depended upon an unprecedented bull run between 1982 and 1997. During that period, the stock market went up fourteen out of sixteen years and the average annual return was almost 15 percent.

From 1967 to 1982, however, the value of the annual Dow Jones average dropped seven out of fifteen years. Over the entire period, the average increased by a total of only five points, from 879 to 884. That equates to an average increase of about .35 points per year and an average annual return of approximately 0.04 percent.

Two thousand dollars invested in the Dow Jones in mid-1967 would have been worth about $2,012 by mid-1982. If the same $2,000 had been invested in a bond fund with an average return of 7 percent, it would have been worth approximately $5,415 in 1982.

Over the entire thirty-year period between 1967 and 1997, the Dow Jones composite went up by an average of about 8 percent per year. In its worst year, from the last trading day in December 1973 to the last trading day in December 1974, the Dow Jones average actually dropped from 824 to 596, a loss of a bit more than 27 percent. Fifteen years later, the Dow Jones went up by 27 percent. If those had been consecutive years, however, the result would have been a net loss, and a clear lesson on the cost of volatility. That is because 1.27 times .73 is only .93.

Over the same thirty years, Moody's Aaa bonds yielded from 5.51 percent to 14.17 percent, an average return of more than 9 percent with much lower volatility than stocks. But the last sixteen years still heavily favored stocks, despite three years of negative returns.

No one knows what will happen in the next thirty years, but regardless of the relative performance of stocks and bonds, saving and investing will be manifestly superior to doing neither.

However, if you start late, you have little chance of winning, and, if you gamble to catch up, then you risk losing more ground than you may gain. Eventually, either error could deposit your "Golden Years" in a tin can.

Gambling

"Fattenin' hogs ain't in luck."

—JOEL CHANDLER HARRIS

Whether it is the thrill of victory, the prospect of instant wealth, or just the fun of it, millions gamble, gamble frequently, and gamble big. One would presume, therefore, that most of them win. They don't. The entire gaming industry—the big casinos, the thousands of employees, the tens of thousands of machines, the glitzy advertisements, and the vast neon signs—is built on their losses.

In fact, the gambling industry exists on a singular premise: You probably lose. Every single game is constructed to ensure it over the long run. If you bet on a professional football game, for instance, you must bet $11 to win $10. The bookmaker has no interest in whether you win or lose the bet, he just wants to ensure that the same amount of money is bet on each team. So he manages the point spread to ensure equality of "action." Thus, by game day, if

1,000 gamblers have bet on one team, then 1,000 have bet the other way. The next day, there will be 1001 winners: the 1,000 gamblers who were lucky enough to bet on the winning team, each of whom will have won $10, and the bookmaker, who will have "won" $1,000.

If you bet on sixteen football games over the course of the season, and if you are smart enough to "beat the spread" nine times, then you will win $13, a 7 percent return on your investment. If you lose nine of sixteen, then you will lose $29, or more than 16 percent. Either way, the bookmaker will get $16.

Casino poker works in a similar fashion. In return for providing a fair deal, the dealer keeps, or "drags," a small percentage of each pot. After a while, this adds up. If the average pot is $50 and the average drag is 2 percent, then after 100 hands the dealer will have dragged $100. In other words, he will have "won" the equivalent of two pots—and he will have lost zero pots. If you and your opponents play long enough, the dealer will eventually get all of the money on the table. For the players, the only evidence of superior skill will be the order of insolvency.

Slot machines can be faster. The house "edge" on them can exceed 10 percent, but even at a house edge of 5 percent, death can be swift. Suppose you sit down to a new-age, dollar slot machine with $100 worth of $1 casino coins. Since the latest machines are fully electronic, it is easy to play at least six times per minute. And you can play up to three dollars at a time, an opportunity you cannot pass up. After ten minutes, you should be down by about $9. After an hour, you should have about $46 left. You will probably not make it to the end of the second hour unless you replenish your stake, which is what most tourists do.

Roulette, craps, twenty-one, baccarat, the racetrack, the lottery, and all other forms of gambling have the same thing in common. Each and every one of them is set up to ensure that the game provider wins. If you have ever seen the casinos in Las Vegas, all of which have been built on the losses of people who gamble there, then you know that the people who provide the games have gotten pretty good at it.

Still, it is okay to gamble—as long as you do not harbor the delusion that you are likely to win. Once you can accept the likelihood of loss, then you can treat gambling as a form of entertainment (or as an atypically entertaining form of taxation, since all states that permit gambling also tax it).

Almost all forms of entertainment cost money. Readers pay for books. Bird-watchers pay for binoculars and cameras. Even hikers pay for boots. In all cases, the cost is absolute. Whatever the entertainee pays is gone for good.

Gambling is the exception, because gamblers will often get back some portion of the money that they originally wagered. They may also get the same amount back or even, in rare instances, more than they wagered. Thus, gambling is the only form of entertainment that offers its participating audience the opportunity, however remote, of finishing the evening with more money than they had at its beginning.

Gambling is, in fact, a form of entertainment. It is not a road to big money. Only a few players win; the majority lose. The business of gambling, which is very big money, has been statistically structured to guarantee it.

If you decide to gamble, do it for fun. You may defeat the house advantage in the short run with a streak of good luck, but you should expect to lose in the long run. It's the safest bet you can make.

26

Streaks and the Law of Averages

"I feel like a fugitive from the law of averages."

—BILL MAULDIN

Streaks occur when the same unlikely event happens over and over, or much more often than logic would seem to tolerate. Over the long run, however, good streaks and bad streaks tend to balance each other out. The sum of these streaks, both good and bad, is called the Law of Averages.

Most of us have experienced many streaks firsthand, although we seem to dwell on the bad ones: the week that both the washing machine and the furnace went out, the two flat tires on the same day-trip to the theme park, the season when our favorite baseball player went hitless in twenty consecutive at bats, the police fund-raiser where we lost ten consecutive hands of blackjack.

As illogical as they may seem, though, streaks are fundamental to the disorder of Nature. That's because the opposite of streaks, which is perfect order, is usually contrary to the nature of Nature.

Shuffle ten red cards and ten blue cards together at least ten times. The total number of cards in the randomly combined deck is twenty. If they are in perfect order, then the cards will alternate in color: red, blue, red, blue, red, blue, et cetera. But this isn't what happens. That is because the odds of a perfect, alternating sequence of color are less than one in 92,000 ($1 \times 10/19 \times 9/18 \times 9/17 \times 8/16 \ldots$).

Of course, any sequence of same-colored cards might be more than just two in a row. For instance, the odds that the first five cards in the twenty-card deck will all be the same color, which would be quite a streak, are approximately 1 in 31 (the chances that the second card will be the same color as the first are 9 in 19, the odds of the third card being the same color as the first two are 8 in 18, the fourth card's odds are 7 in 17, and the fifth card's odds are 6 in 16). Therefore, a five-card streak of either color at the beginning of the deck, which is a streak, turns out to be about three thousand times more likely than a "normal" alternating sequence of twenty cards.

In general, streaks are more likely than order. A baseball player who bats .250 will not get a hit every fourth trip to the plate. (If this were always true, then the batter would be walked intentionally every fourth at bat.) Instead, his or her hits will tend to come in bunches. Sometimes the bunches will extend into streaks. On other occasions, the lack of hits will become a streak. The chances that a .250 hitter will go hitless in twenty consecutive trips to the plate, for instance, are only about 3 in 1,000. That is a nasty streak. But if the batter has six hundred at bats per year, then he is likely to endure just such a streak almost twice per season.

The same thing can happen to you. If you have a 49 percent chance of winning any hand of blackjack at the local police fund-raiser, then you would not expect to lose ten hands in a row—a horrible streak of bad luck. In fact, the odds are about 1 in 840. But if 250 people play fifty hands of blackjack at the police fund-raiser every year, then, on average, fifteen of them will lose ten consecutive hands. One unlucky player may lose fourteen in a row.

In the natural disorder of Nature, events tend to occur in bunches. Streaks, therefore, are fundamental to life. If you must choose between a streak or order in the short run, always pick the streak. But be careful. It is often easy to determine which streak has just occurred, but you can never be certain how long any streak will last.

Women, it seems, intuitively understand the inevitability of streaks. Cecilia Sharpe, who won ten consecutive hands of blackjack at the annual Snohomish County Law Enforcement fund-raiser several years ago, then promptly quit, is an excellent example.

Men, on the other hand, seem to be more inclined toward the Law of Averages. Reginald DeNiall is a good example. He manages to lose money at craps, a dice game, at the Snohomish fund-raiser each and every year without fail. Last year, he asked Cecilia, whom he has known for many years and who seems to win at the annual Law Enforcement fund-raiser more often than she loses, to help him out.

After some gentle cajoling, Cecilia agreed. Then she looked Reginald right in the eye and said that she could show him how to win 70 percent of the time.

GEORGE SHAFFNER · 137

Every experienced gambler knows that there is no such thing as a system that can reverse unfavorable odds, much less produce a winning percentage of as much as 70 percent. That knowledge, and the inescapable reality of his own gambling career, caused Reginald to be skeptical in the extreme. Nevertheless, he asked Cecilia to explain her system.

Rather than explain it, Cecilia offered to prove it. She then removed her Sharp (no relation) calculator from her purse, along with a pencil and paper, and went to work. Reginald did his part by agreeing that any experienced craps player should win at least 48 percent of the time by avoiding long-shot bets.

With that figure in mind, and assuming a population of 1,000 craps bettors and an even bet of $10 per player per roll of the dice, Cecilia modeled the following result:

1. On the first roll of the dice, 480 players win $10 each. All of them immediately retire from the game as winners.

2. The other 520 lose the first bet. However, 120 of them win the next two bets in a row (520 × .48 × .48), leaving them ahead $10. They also retire from the game.

3. After three rolls, four hundred players remain in the game. Of that number, approximately 259 have lost two of three. But the other 141 have lost all three rolls and they are also asked to retire from the game.

4. Sixty of the remaining 259 (approximately 23 percent) win the next two rolls, after which they retire ahead. Of the remaining 199, seventy (approximately 27 percent) have lost three of four and they are asked

to retire from the game. The remaining 129 (slightly less than 50 percent) have won two and lost three of the first five rolls and they are allowed to play on.

5. Thirty of the remaining 129 win both rolls six and seven, after which they retire ahead. Thirty-five lose both rolls and retire as losers, leaving sixty-four players to continue, all of whom have won three rolls and lost four.

6. Of the sixty-four players who continue, fifteen win the next two rolls and retire ahead and seventeen lose both rolls and retire after winning three rolls and losing six.

7. After nine rolls, 705 players have quit the game ahead $10. Another 263 have quit the game after falling behind by exactly $30. The remaining thirty-two players have won four rolls and lost five, so there are a total of 295 losers.

8. Although there are 705 winners and only 295 losers, and no loser has lost more than $30, the house is still ahead by more than $1,100, as follows:

Number of Losers	Total Losses
263	$7,890
32	$320
Total Losses	**$8,210**
Less Winnings	$7,050
House Advantage	**$1,160**

Thus, Cecilia proved that it is possible for there to be more than 700 winners out of 1,000 players, even though the house holds a clear advantage.

As a former CEO and a sitting congressman, however, Reginald featured himself as a high-profile player. He did not, therefore, see the point of quitting after only a few rolls of the dice. So he asked Cecilia what his bottom line was likely to be after 100 bets of $100 each. Cecilia quickly informed him that, according to the Law of Averages, he would be $400 in the red after winning forty-eight bets and losing fifty-two. However, depending on his streaks, he could either be ahead—or much farther behind. As was his nature, Reginald chose the Law of Averages and probable loss.

In the short run, streaks are indigenous to the Nature of numbers. Over the long run, however, the sum of all streaks normalizes into the Law of Averages. Whether you watch or whether you play, expect the streak. But don't expect it to last because, sooner or later, the Law of Averages will have its day.

27

Coincidence

*"There is no excellent beauty that hath not
some strangeness in the proportion."*

—FRANCIS BACON

If coincidences are so rare, how can they be so common?
The answer, it turns out, can be found in the simple ag-
gregation of daily experience.

Given the tremendous power of our senses, it is not
much of a stretch to estimate that we see an average of at
least one new thing per second, especially if we include all
of the people we see, all of the buildings and trees and
shrubs, all of the cars, all of the parts of cars like license
plates, and so on and so on and so on. Likewise, unless im-
paired, we ought to hear or touch or smell at least one new
something per second.

The average sentient American adult is awake an average
of about 16.5 hours per day, which is 990 minutes or
59,400 seconds. That adds up to a conservative estimate of

around 118,800 (2 × 59,400) observations or experiences per day. Out of so many, some are certain to be rare.

On the way to work last week, Cecilia Sharpe saw two Porsche 911s in a row on the Interstate. A fan of the famous German marque, Cecilia pulled closer to look them both over. One was a white, turbocharged model from the mid-eighties; the other a red, late-nineties convertible. There were no Porsche dealerships in the immediate area. The license plates were from different states. The drivers left the interstate at different exits so they weren't traveling together.

Fifteen to sixteen million new vehicles are purchased in the United States every year. In 1998, however, Porsche sold only about 8,000 911s. Porsche sales have been even lower in the past, but they tend to be driven much longer than the average automobile. So Porsche 911s can be approximated to be about one in every two thousand cars on the road in the United States. Therefore, Cecilia's odds of seeing two in a row at any one time were about one in four million (1 in 2,000 × 1 in 2,000), which she thought to be an extraordinary coincidence.

Being numerically inclined, however, she began to think it over during the rest of her trip to work in downtown Seattle. That evening, on her one-hour commute home in stop-and-go traffic, she counted more than six thousand cars traveling either with her or in the opposite direction. Since she faced the same quantity of traffic twice each day, she concluded that she saw a million cars every eighty-three to eighty-four workdays, or about every 3.6 months. Approximately every fourteen and a half months, therefore, and a total of perhaps thirty-three times over the course of her career, Cecilia would be likely to see two consecutive

Porsches on the road. From that perspective, the extraordinary coincidence of the consecutive Porsche 911s seemed a bit more ordinary.

Surprised by the ease of the explanation, Cecilia decided to apply the same logic to those mysterious airport encounters with old friends and acquaintances. First, she estimated that she knew at least one thousand people in the United States. She also estimated that she traveled by air twenty times per year, passing through an average of six airports per trip, three each way. At each airport, Cecilia estimated that she saw an average of two thousand travelers, even if she was just changing planes on the same concourse at a hub like Chicago, San Francisco, or Denver.

Therefore, every year Cecilia saw approximately 240,000 people at airports, about one in every 1,100 people living in the United States. In the aggregate of her life's experience, however, Cecilia estimated that she had known more than 1,000 Americans well enough to recognize them. So, all things being equal, she concluded that she would unexpectedly encounter an acquaintance at an airport once every twelve or thirteen months.

By the same logic, if you see, hear, smell, or touch 118,800 things every day, then something you experience every eight or nine days will be, on average, a one in a million coincidence. It may be something very small, so you may not notice it. On occasion, it will be worthy of note. In a rare moment, it may truly be something extraordinary. If you experience or observe 118,800 events per day, then you are likely to encounter a one in a billion coincidence every twenty-three years or so.

Coincidences are common in life. Their frequency is a function of the thousands of things that we experience every waking hour of the day. Thus, they are a product of our senses, which are Nature's gift to us. Even though coincidences are not rare, it behooves us to observe each one and to be thankful to Nature for what each coincidence represents: one sensational experience in a lifetime of billions!

28

THE PLLO

"Yet in my walks it seems to me
That the Grace of God is in courtesy."

—HILAIRE BELLOC

Despite the famous weather, the Northwest is not a perfect place to live. One of the reasons is rapidly increasing traffic congestion. As usual, local politicians are steadfastly ignoring the situation. But the problem, especially during rush hours, is often complicated by drivers who insist on driving in the passing lane regardless of their slow speed.

This is no coincidence; there are just too many of them. Therefore, we must conclude that this phenomenon is directly attributable to the emergence of a covert road conspiracy called the PLLO, which stands for Permanent Left Lane Occupants. Thought to have been founded in the Seattle area in the late 1980s, the PLLO movement has since spread to almost every state in the nation, possibly with the financial backing of a secret, right wing, government agency.

These days, you can observe the PLLO in action on any

stretch of Washington highway at almost any time of the day or night. Members are immediately recognizable by their modus operandi, which is so consistent that it must certainly require in-depth training:

- First, the PLL Occupant pulls slowly onto the freeway.
- Second, he or she moves immediately into the left-most lane.
- Once in control of the passing lane, he or she drops to a speed that is five to ten miles per hour slower than the prevailing pace of traffic prior to his or her arrival.
- He or she remains in the left lane at the slower speed for the duration of their drive.

When traveling in pairs, committed PLLO members have even been known to leave the High Occupancy Vehicle lane to slow traffic in the passing lane. And they can sometimes be observed driving the exact same speed as the driver to their immediate right for miles.

The result is always the same. Lines of cars begin to form behind them. Clumps of traffic appear on otherwise uncongested highways. If there are enough PLLO on the road, as there frequently are in the Puget Sound area, then the clumps begin to congeal into PLLO-induced traffic jams. Faster drivers, who have been denied the passing lane by the PLLO, become impatient and then angry. Dangerous driving tactics, such as tailgating and passing on the right, inevitably ensue.

If a single PLL Occupant manages to impede ten cars by a minute each, let's say, then the total loss is only ten minutes and tempers are likely to remain in check. But the hard-core PLLO are not visitors to the left-hand lane, they are inhabitants. If an ardent PLLO commuter can delay one hundred cars by an average of three minutes each way, then the daily loss will be ten hours per day and the aggregate annual delay will be 2,500 hours. That equates to more than 300 workdays of wasted road time per year per practicing PLL Occupant. If someone misses a job interview or is late for an important sales call, or if an accident is caused by someone who is in too much of a hurry to get around the PLLO, then the potential loss can be much larger.

No one knows why so many ordinary citizens have volunteered for active duty with the PLLO. Possibly, they believe that slower traffic is safer traffic, even if too many cars are following much too closely and others are being passed on the right where the blind spot is most severe. Perhaps the PLLO want to live life in the fast lane, even if they don't have the speed. Maybe they believe that it is their right to drive in the left-hand lane, regardless of the impact on fellow drivers.

However, there is an actual cost incurred by the act of moving out of the left lane so that others can pass. If, for instance, an average PLL Occupant is driving at 50 miles per hour, then he (or she) will travel about 220 feet every three seconds. If the PLL Occupant takes three seconds to move fifteen feet to the right to get out of the way of faster traffic, then, by the Pythagorean Theorem,* the net dis-

---

* According to Pythagoras, the length of the hypotenuse of a right triangle squared is equal to the total of the lengths of the other two sides squared. The 220 feet traveled while moving into the right lane is the hypotenuse, which is 48,400 when squared. The short side of the triangle is the 15 feet in distance from the left lane to the right lane, which is 225 when squared. To get the third side of the triangle, which is the net forward distance traveled, we subtract 225 from 48,400 to get 48,175. Then we take its square root, which is 219.49 feet. That means that the PLL Occupant will have traveled 6.12 inches (.51 feet) less toward his destination by virtue of the detour into the right-hand lane.

tance traveled will be only about 219.5 feet. The other six inches will be consumed in moving into the adjacent lane.

So our sample PLL Occupant will have been delayed by the time it takes to cover a distance of six inches. At fifty miles per hour, that equates to a time loss of approximately .007 seconds. If the PLLO moves back into the left-hand lane after faster traffic has passed, then the total time loss is .014 seconds.*

It takes just 0.014 seconds to get out of the way. Therefore, something like one-seventieth of a second is a fairly reasonable estimate of the cost of highway courtesy. It means that seventy similar acts of highway courtesy will take a total of one second.

Most acts of courtesy take more time, but not much more. A door can be opened in a second or two. A plastic container can be picked up and thrown in a proper receptacle in a few more. It may take ten or fifteen seconds to let a pedestrian cross the road.

But the return on a few seconds of courtesy can be significant. People, perhaps a lot of people, will get where they are going sooner and more safely. The landscape will be less dangerous and more appealing to the eye. Occasionally, someone may even get the impression that someone else cares, even if it's only for 0.014 seconds.

---

*A car traveling 50 miles per hour covers 264,000 feet per hour (50 times 5,280). That is equivalent to 73.33 feet per second (by dividing by the number of seconds in an hour, which is 3,600). Thus, at 50 miles per hour, 6.12 inches is traveled in approximately .007 seconds.

CHAPTER

29

The Tailgater's Advantage

"As if there were safety in stupidity alone."

—HENRY DAVID THOREAU

According to the National Safety Council, there were 10.7 million automobile accidents in the United States in 1995. More than 1.4 million of them resulted in disabling injury or death. Rear-end collisions accounted for about one in every six accidents, or more than 1.7 million accidents every year, many of them of the disabling variety, some of them fatal.

Rear-enders ought to be among the easiest of accidents to eliminate since drivers need to do no more than follow each other at a safe distance. But tailgating seems to be growing in popularity, so there must be a payoff.

The California Department of Motor Vehicles recommends a minimum following distance of three seconds for any vehicle. At a speed of sixty miles an hour, that equates to 264 feet, or around 16 car lengths. But Billy Ray DeNiall, Reginald's younger son and a model tailgater, routinely cuts that distance by two-thirds, to only 88 feet. He must have excellent reflexes because he has just one second—instead of three—to observe any dramatic change in the vehicle in front of him, then decide what to do, and then get it done.

If Billy Ray were a typically cautious driver, he would have a fifteen-minute commute to school. However, as a result of his courageous tailgating, Billy Ray now gets to school two full seconds sooner. Therefore, he has reduced his daily commute time to an economical twenty-nine minutes and fifty-six seconds, an impressive savings of two-tenths of 1 percent.

Now we know the tailgater's advantage. But do we know what the real risk is?

In the real world, there may be many occasions when not even one second of reaction time is available to the committed tailgater. That's because vehicles have variable stopping distances. In tests of more than 200 vehicles, the magazine *Motor Trend* reports stopping distances from 60 miles per hour that vary from as little as 102 feet (a Toyota sports car) to as much as 167 feet (a Dodge pickup truck). (Those figures were for new vehicles, almost all of which had antilock brakes and were in perfect repair. Older vehicles, especially pickup trucks, vans, and SUVs, can take more than 200 feet to stop from 60 miles per hour, and more yet if their brakes are worn.)

If Billy Ray has the misfortune to close in on the Toyota in his Dodge pickup, he will no longer have even a second to react. That is because it will take his vehicle about sixty-five feet longer to stop than the vehicle in front of him. In fact, Billy Ray's reaction time will be reduced to .26 seconds! That is too little time to have any hope of evading collision. Sadly, Billy Ray is more likely to rear-end the Toyota at as much as thirty miles per hour, a speed at which collisions can be fatal.

Most weekends, you can see plenty of nose-to-tail driving at any automobile race. Called "drafting," it provides an aerodynamic advantage to both the leading and trailing drivers. But drafting is done only in a highly controlled race environment, all of the drivers are skilled professionals, they drive homogeneous and specially prepared automobiles, and there is a crew of highly trained mechanics standing by all the time to make sure that everything is working as well as possible. Even so, hardly a race goes by without serious accident, which is why there is usually a mobile medical team on site.

In normal driving, there is no advantage to drafting, aerodynamic or otherwise. The streets are filled with amateur, distracted, and disinterested drivers. Their vehicles span a broad spectrum of specification and performance. Many of the vehicles are old, many are in a poor state of repair, and pit crews and medical teams are not standing by.

Even though they have less to lose, old people rarely tailgate. That is because they have had to learn the rules of risk and return in order to become old people. One of those rules is: Unless under gunpoint, never take a 20,000-to-one long shot.

Tailgating is the twentieth-century archetype of the dimwit decision. The upside is tiny; two seconds or so. If you tailgate to and from work every day for fifty years, including weekends, then you can save a total of about 73,000 seconds, or around twenty hours.

If you are twenty-five years old and you expect to live to be seventy-five, then a fatal rear-ender could cost you more than 1.57 billion seconds of breath, which is more than 438,000 hours. The downside is 21,000 times the upside. The downside is that you could lose your life.

PART

4

Dark Matters

*"There are more things in heaven and earth, Horatio,
than are dreamt of in your philosophy."*

—WILLIAM SHAKESPEARE

Death by Misadventure

*"Carriages without horses shall go,
And accidents fill the world with woe."*

—ANONYMOUS

All human beings have fears. As if Nature hasn't supplied us with enough of them, such as hurricanes, killer bees, and *e. coli*, we have invented many more. Assault weapons, nuclear waste, Jet Skis, garbage disposals, and fast food come immediately to mind. Because there are so many natural and man-made dangers out there, and because we are reminded of them with such regularity by our chums in the media, one of the commonest fears of our time is that we will die before our time.

Statistics compiled by the National Center of Injury Prevention Control (which is a relatively new part of the National Centers for Disease Control) show that this fear is not completely unfounded. In each of the years from 1993 through 1995, the first three years in which mortal injury results were compiled by the CDC, 151,000 Americans, plus or minus 74, died from firearms, traffic accidents, poisoning, suffocation, drowning, falls, fire, machinery, over-exertion, and other causes.

In the same three-year period, the total number of deaths in the United States averaged very near 2.3 million annually according to the National Funeral Directors Association. So, from 1993 to 1995, about 6.6 percent of those who expired, or about one in fifteen, did so "before their time":

Year	U.S. Population	Deaths	Deaths by Misadventure	Percent
1993	257,796,000	2,268,000	151,074	6.66%
1994	260,372,000	2,286,000	150,940	6.60%
1995	262,890,000	2,309,000	151,033	6.54%

One chance in fifteen is not a huge probability. But it is significant. If you are lucky enough to live to be eighty years old, then about 12,000,000 people will die from homicide, suicide, and accident within your lifetime. Moreover, each one of them will lose an average of 23.9 years of potential life.*

Therefore, if you are unlucky enough to die by misadventure, then you are likely to forgo some 30 percent of your life expectancy. It could be more, especially if you are male. So it would seem prudent to determine what you may be able to do to minimize your chances of an unexpected or violent end.

---

*In 1995, the 151,033 unfortunate souls who died before their time lost an aggregate of 3,609,454 years of potential life, which is an average of 23.9 each.

Without question, the very best way to reduce the likelihood of an untimely death is to be a woman. Even if you were not born a woman, then you may wish to consider behaving like one. Presumably, this would mean doing the little things, like reading the label on the bottle before mixing your heart medicine with bourbon, or not swimming across the flood-swollen river when the water temperature is only fifty degrees Fahrenheit (ten degrees on the centigrade scale) just to prove that you can do it, or not relying on lethal weapons to resolve differences of opinion.

Whatever it is that women do and men don't, or vice versa, women lead less perilous lives. From 1993 to 1995, women, who made up slightly more than half of the population, accounted for only 29 percent of all deaths by accident, homicide, and suicide:

Year	Deaths by Misadventure	Men	Women	Percent Women
1993	151,074	107,948	43,126	28.55%
1994	150,940	107,914	43,026	28.51%
1995	151,033	107,126	43,907	29.07%

In all three years, and presumably in most of the years before that, men were more than twice as likely as women to die before their time. Apparently, this was no accident. In 1995, men were more than three times as likely to die by homicide and more than four times as likely to die by their own hand:

Category	Male Deaths	Female Deaths	Ratio M to F
Accident	61,497	31,997	1.92 to 1
Homicide	17,408	5,144	3.38 to 1
Suicide	25,392	5,915	4.29 to 1
Other	2,829	851	3.32 to 1
Totals	**107,126**	**43,907**	**2.44 to 1**

At a more detailed level of misadventure, forthrightly labeled cause of death, women were also less likely to die in every major category:

Cause of Death	Total Deaths	Male Deaths	Female Deaths	Ratio M to F
Motor Vehicle	43,495	29,270	14,225	2.1 to 1
Firearms	35,700	30,475	5,225	5.8 to 1
Poisoning	14,269	10,054	4,215	2.4 to 1
Falls	11,217	6,349	4,868	1.3 to 1
Suffocation	10,305	7,055	3,250	2.2 to 1
Drowning	4,827	3,826	1,001	3.8 to 1
Fire/Burn	4,268	2,529	1,739	1.5 to 1
Other	26,952	17,568	9,384	1.9 to 1

Not all of the news is bad for men all of the time, though. In one age bracket, eighty and older, women are more likely than men to die by misadventure. The reason, of course, is that the majority of men are already dead, especially the risk takers. In all of the younger age brackets except two, men are two to four times as likely as women to die an untimely death:

Age Bracket	Male Deaths	Female Deaths	Ratio M to F
0 to 9	3,374	2,345	1.44 to 1
10 to 19	11,011	3,651	3.02 to 1
20 to 29	22,030	5,068	4.35 to 1
30 to 39	21,326	6,349	3.36 to 1
40 to 49	16,311	5,182	3.15 to 1
50 to 59	8,970	3,291	2.73 to 1
60 to 69	7,489	3,369	2.22 to 1
70 to 79	8,138	5,193	1.57 to 1
80+	8,187	9,355	0.88 to 1
Unspecified	290	104	2.79 to 1
Totals	107,126	43,907	2.44 to 1

By now, a fairly clear course has been charted for those seeking to minimize the possibility of an untimely demise. Although some factors may be generally beyond your control, such as being booked on the *Titanic* on her maiden voyage, there are a few simple precautions that can dramatically improve your odds of dying of heart disease or cancer, both of which are considered to be natural causes. Those most likely to be effective are:

1. If you are male, then behaving like a woman in matters of risk could reduce your odds of premature death by almost 60 percent (from about 107,663 per year to about 43,353). Moreover, if every man could do this faithfully every single day, then the national death toll by misadventure would be cut from about 151,000 to around 87,000 per year, a decrease of more than 42 percent.

2. If you are already a woman, or if you are a man and you cannot bring yourself to act like a woman, then pretend to be old. Older people, especially those in their sixties, are more cautious than younger people. If you are a man in your twenties, this simple leap of conservatism could cut your chances of an untimely end by as much as 66 percent (100 percent—[7,489 ÷ 22,030]), which would be nearly as effective as acting like a woman. (A male in his twenties who behaved exactly like a female in her twenties would cut his chances of premature death by 77 percent, which is equal to 100 percent—[5,068 ÷ 22,030].)

3. If you consider gender to be fate rather than choice, and if you insist on acting your age, then at least stay out of range. In 1995, 35,279 Americans died from gunshots, which was almost 24 percent of all deaths by misadventure. Of those, more than half were by suicide.

4. If you must assert your Constitutional right to carry one of the nation's 200 million guns, then at least refuse to commit suicide with it, or by any other means. This singular act of personal hygiene could reduce your chances of early death by 21 percent (31,307 ÷ 151,033).

5. Regardless of your sex and age, do whatever you can to avoid being murdered. Homicides accounted for about 15 percent of all deaths by misadventure in 1995 (22,552 ÷ 151,033).

6. Do not drive while intoxicated or travel in the company of those who commit this crime. If everyone, men and women alike, could cooperate in this one endeavor, then assuming that at least 40 percent of all

fatal traffic accidents are caused by drunk drivers, deaths from misadventure could be reduced by more than 11 percent (43,495 $\times$ .4 $\div$ 151,033) per year.

Of course, nobody can completely eliminate the possibility of death by misadventure. There are too many dangers in life, and the day-to-day living of it requires that we encounter too many of them too often for all of us to be safe all of the time. However, by doing just a few simple things, you can significantly increase the probability that you will live a long, long time.

CHAPTER

31

Life Expectancy

*"Hello darkness, my old friend
I've come to talk with you again."*

—PAUL SIMON

A baby born in the United States in the year 1900 had a life expectancy of about forty-eight years. By 1998, this figure had increased to about seventy-seven years, which is a testimony to advances in diet, hygiene, education, medicine, and a thousand technologies. It may also be something of a puzzlement to anyone who is older than seventy-seven and not dead yet.

The solution to the puzzle is that life expectancy at birth and life expectancy later in life are two entirely different matters. Cecilia Sharpe is a fine example. According to the National Center for Health Statistics, a baby born in the United States in 1950, the year of Cecilia's birth, could expect to live until the age of sixty-eight. However, Cecilia's life expectancy is not age sixty-eight. Nor is it the current figure of seventy-seven. There are several reasons why:

1. The life expectancy estimate of seventy-seven years is an average figure which applies only to babies born in the United States in 1998.
2. Cecilia is a woman, which means that she is likely to outlive the average by three years (men live about three years less than the average, women about three years more than the average).
3. Cecilia is not dead yet. Unfortunately, a lot of people born in 1950 already are dead. Their deaths were factored into the original life expectancy estimate of sixty-eight years for people born that year. Since they died before age sixty-eight, and since age sixty-eight was an average, then they allowed others to die after the age of sixty-eight.
4. So, since Cecilia has not died, her life expectancy has increased considerably beyond the initial estimate.

In fact, according to the Life Expectancy Tables from the U.S. Internal Revenue Service, people who were born in 1950 and who were still alive in 1998 had an average life expectancy of age eighty-three, a fifteen-year advance over their expectancy at birth. Since Cecilia is female, her current life expectancy is closer to eighty-six years, which means that the most likely year of her death is the year 2036.

Cecilia's estranged husband is not likely to be so lucky. He was born in 1948, just two years before Cecilia. But he is a male and he is a smoker. That means that his life expectancy is more likely to be around seventy-six years, which is his current age of fifty, plus thirty-four years for being not dead yet, but minus three years for being male and minus another five years for being a habitual smoker. Thus, the mostly likely year of his death is predicted to be the year 2024, twelve years before Cecilia and, in Gwendolyn Sharpe's mind, perhaps a small measure of justice.

But Gwen's father is still not likely to die in the year 2024, and her mother is not likely to die in the year 2036 either. That is because according to actuarial tables published by Faber and Wade, there is no year in which death is as likely as continued life, at least until the age of 115. Until that time, the probability of death occurring in any one year varies from a low of 0.009 percent (about one chance in 11,000) for a girl of age eleven to a high of 46.5 percent for either gender at age 114. In most of the years in between, the odds that a man will die in any given year are two to three times as high as they are for a woman of the same age:

Age	Odds of Male Death	Odds of Female Death	Ratio M to F
0	00.844%	00.664%	1.27 to 1
10	00.013%	00.010%	1.30 to 1
20	00.140%	00.050%	2.80 to 1
30	00.153%	00.050%	3.06 to 1
40	00.193%	00.095%	2.03 to 1
50	00.567%	00.305%	1.86 to 1
60	01.299%	00.792%	1.64 to 1
70	03.473%	01.764%	1.97 to 1
80	07.644%	03.966%	1.93 to 1
90	15.787%	11.250%	1.40 to 1
100	26.876%	23.969%	1.12 to 1
110	39.770%	39.043%	1.02 to 1

If, for instance, Gwen's father can make it to age eighty, then his odds of making it to age eighty-one are better than 92 percent (100 percent—7.644 percent = 92.356 percent). In order to reach eighty, though, he will probably have to quit smoking and start exercising. On the other hand, if Cecilia can make it to age eighty, then her odds of getting to age eighty-one are better than 96 percent. And she doesn't smoke.

According to the National Funeral Directors Association, about 2,294,000 people died in the year 1997. Presumably, none of them was you. Although the annual American death toll will rise to approximately 3,472,000 in the year 2030, the odds are against your death in any one of those years, at least until you reach the age of 115, after which your odds of death in any one year are about 50/50 until the actual event.

However, the accumulation of the odds of death are still likely to prevent you from reaching 115. If you were a woman born in 1933 like Gwen's aunt Flora, for instance, then you were sixty-five years old in 1998, and the odds that you would die in 1999 were just 1.26 percent. But the chances that you would die the following year were 1.37 percent, and 1.48 percent the year after that. After a while, all of those small percentages begin to add up, as follows:

Aunt Flora's Age	Odds of Death in That Year	Odds Flora Won't Die	Cumulative Odds of Flora's Survival
65	1.259%	98.741%	98.741%
66	1.372%	98.628%	97.386%
67	1.476%	98.524%	95.949%
68	1.573%	98.427%	94.440%
69	1.664%	98.336%	92.868%
70	1.764%	98.236%	91.230%
71	1.883%	98.117%	89.512%
72	2.021%	97.979%	87.703%

73	2.183%	97.817%	85.788%
74	2.369%	97.631%	83.756%
75	2.588%	97.412%	81.589%
76	2.834%	97.166%	79.276%
77	3.091%	96.909%	76.826%

All things being equal, Aunt Flora has a better than three in four chance of living to exceed the average life expectancy of babies born in 1998. However, Aunt Flora cannot be expected to live to age 115, when her chances of dying in a single year are about 50 percent. That is because her future odds of death will continue to accumulate:

Aunt Flora's Age	Odds of Death in That Year	Odds Flora Won't Die	Cumulative Odds of Flora's Survival
77	3.091%	96.909%	76.826%
78	3.355%	96.645%	74.248%
79	3.640%	96.360%	71.546%
80	3.966%	96.034%	68.708%
81	4.353%	95.647%	65.717%
82	4.815%	95.185%	62.553%
83	5.363%	94.637%	59.198%
84	5.994%	94.006%	55.650%
85	6.699%	93.301%	51.922%
86	7.472%	92.528%	48.042%

When Aunt Flora actually succumbs is a matter of specu-lation. To a large extent, it will be dependent on her age and her genetic makeup. But it will also be a matter of diet, habit, exercise, and frame of mind, meaning that Flora will have the opportunity to influence her life expectancy to a considerable extent. This is an opportunity that we all share. If, for instance, you wish to die sooner than your birth-year counterparts, then you might consider:

1. being a man, especially with a history of heart disease in the immediate family;
2. becoming obese and staying that way;
3. smoking cigarettes with regularity and abusing alcohol and other drugs;
4. choosing a high-stress occupation, such as a criminal or inner-city arms dealer; and
5. having unprotected sex with as many people as possible.

Life, however, is a gift. If you wish to honor the gift by living life to its fullest, which even the lowliest of sea creatures are intelligent enough to do, then you might consider:

1. being or behaving like a woman (see "Death by Misadventure");
2. eating a balanced diet rich in water, vitamins, minerals, and fiber;
3. exercising regularly;
4. getting an annual medical checkup; and
5. owning pets (especially cuddly ones), which lowers the blood pressure of their owners and provides a general sense of well-being.

If you choose to work at postponing your death, then you have a decent chance of living beyond the age of eighty-five. In 1990, there were three million Americans who had surpassed that advanced age. By 1998, the total had increased to more than four million.

All over the world, people are living longer than at any time in the history of man. You are likely (although not certain) to live longer than your parents, who probably lived longer than their parents. Your children are likely (but not certain) to live longer than you. It is, in fact, quite possible that your lifetime will span six generations:

Generation (Oldest)	Age at Death	Year of Birth	Year of Death
Grandparents	70	1900	1970
Parents	75	1925	2000
You	80	1950	2030
Your Children	85	1975	2060
Your Grandchildren	90	2000	2090
Great Grandchildren	95	2025	2120

Aggregate, six-generation life span: 220 years

Although we may expect our lives to last only eighty years, that may be enough to touch more than two centuries of history. Indeed, there were men and women in the time of the Civil War whose grandparents were alive during the Revolutionary War and whose great-grandchildren may have fought in Korea. That means that they had an opportunity to have a personal discussion with nearly two hundred years of armed conflict.

There are children being born at the end of the twentieth century who should not expect it but who will live to see the dawn of the twenty-second century. Their great-grandparents may have been alive during World War I; their grandparents may have fought in World War II; their

parents may have protested Vietnam. Let us hope, however, that the children of the twenty-first century will have
learned from us, the children of the twentieth, the meaning
of the word futility. If so, then they will mark their time
not by conflict, but by the peaceful advance of the human
spirit.

32

The Preservation of Prejudice

"Rancor is an outpouring of a feeling of inferiority."

—JOSÉ ORTEGA Y GASSET

Prejudice has served our nation well for many, many years. It permitted us to confiscate much of the land we call the United States from its previous inhabitants; it allowed us to establish a large, agrarian economy based upon free labor; it furnished us with the most devastating war in our history; and, to this day, it provides us with a steady diet of distrust, discomfort, hate, fear, and loathing.

Historically, America's best and most persevering prejudices have been founded on skin color. This is no accident. Basing bigotry on race has a number of important advantages:

- Everybody has a skin color.
- Except for a famous exception or two, it is determined at birth.

- It can be seen at a considerable distance.
- For a very long time, we have had a clear majority of one color, which has been the key to the practice of safe prejudice in the United States.
- Skin color is arbitrary—meaning that no reliable inferences on anything of value, including ethic, compassion, or social contribution, can be drawn solely from it.

Actually, the last point is not completely true. The amount of melanin in the skin determines both its color and its owner's ability to resist harm from overexposure to the sun. Basically, the more melanin you have, the better protected you are—and the darker-skinned you are. However, from the perspective of prejudice, which dates back to the Egyptian pharaohs, this is a recent discovery. And it's a pretty minor point.

Otherwise, no study by a responsible academic or government institution has ever been able to prove any general inferiority or superiority of race based on skin color. This is because a generality can be true in math and logic if and only if there are no exceptions. For instance, there are no exceptions to $2 + 2 = 4$. But there are millions of exceptions to "Asian people are smarter than white people." Therefore, no generality can be made, other than "Some Asian people are smarter than some white people, and some white people are smarter than some Asian people."

What has been proven, in general, is that the correlation between the amount of melanin in human skin and the quantity and density of convolutions in the human brain is zero. Zilch. Nada. Nil. So, regardless of your color, you can never tell whether the next person you meet is either smarter or dumber than you are, regardless of their color. The same is true for every other measurable trait known to mankind, and for all of the immeasurable ones as well.

If you are still having a hard time catching on, then perhaps an example will help. If you are a white supremacist, who would you rather invite to your next family barbecue, Colin Powell or John Wayne Gacy? If you are a black supremacist, would you rather invite Gloria Estefan or Idi Amin? If an Asian supremacist, Maya Angelou or Pol Pot? If an Hispanic supremacist, Steven Spielberg or Augusto Pinochet?

The moment you waver, even for a split second, any racial generality is dead.

However, you still can be arbitrary. From the perspective of perpetuation of prejudice, this is critically important. If any form of racial inferiority had ever been proven, then from that moment forward, continued fear and loathing would have been impossible. How could any intelligent being reasonably fear another who had been proven to be weaker or less intelligent? How could any compassionate being reasonably loathe another who was in obvious need of charity and patience?

Luckily, bigotry based upon skin color is about as arbitrary as can be. However, despite its historic advantages, race-based prejudice is beginning to break down. The United States is getting too diverse. It's getting too hard to tell who is what. There are just too many shades of brown.

What are all those East Indians from India? And, by the way, why isn't their skin color more consistent? And what about all those Polynesians? What are they? How about South Americans? Are they Hispanic or Native American or both or something else? What are Arabs: white, cream-colored, beige, sandstone? Are North Africans black or Arab or French or what? What is a Filipino or practically anybody from the Caribbean? And how does one classify a deeply tanned white or Asian person, other than as insufficiently busy?

Worse, the numbers are beginning to deteriorate. America's white majority is in retreat:

Forecast U.S. Racial Composition by Percentage

Year	White	Black	Hispanic	Asian*	Native American
1996	73.3%	12.1%	10.5%	3.4%	0.7%
2000	71.8%	12.2%	11.4%	3.9%	0.7%
2015	66.1%	12.7%	15.1%	5.3%	0.8%
2030	60.5%	13.1%	18.9%	6.6%	0.8%
2050	52.8%	13.6%	24.5%	8.2%	0.9%

*Includes Pacific Islanders

Assuming that the pace of diversity remains constant after 2030, then sometime around two P.M. on October 8, 2057, a date within the life expectancy of almost every American born after 1985, there will be no racial majority in the United States. Every race in this country will be in the minority.

This is a serious arithmetic problem. No prejudice can be safely practiced unless the principal bigots outnumber bigotees (skeptics may wish to research the fate of the British, French, Portuguese, and Spanish colonial empires). Clearly, we need a newer, safer basis for prejudice, and we need it quickly so that we can start reeducating our children as soon as possible.

There is plenty of historical precedent for religious

prejudice, and it is even more arbitrary than prejudice based on skin color. Unfortunately, though, religion can be changed after birth, which unfairly protects the culpable, and, again, there is no clear majority. Also, with a few exceptions, religious preference cannot be identified at a distance with reasonable accuracy. It can be very difficult in Los Angeles, for instance, to tell a lay Protestant from a garden-variety Catholic, or a practicing Hindu from a Buddhist or a Taoist, or a recently converted Zoroastrian from a modern Sikh.

Whatever we choose to replace bias based on skin color, it needs to be easily observed. Eye color isn't a good solution. Contact lenses can be tinted, and really cool people wear sunglasses even at night. For similar reasons, hair color doesn't work very well, and country of origin is even worse than skin color. From fifty yards, how do you tell a Norwegian from a Dane? Or a Brazilian from a Bolivian? Or a Thai from an Indonesian?

Intellect doesn't cut the mustard either. Lots of smart people act stupid. Some stupid people keep their mouths shut, causing practically everyone else to assume they're smart, which may be the case. Even gender doesn't work anymore. These days, it can be hard to determine from a distance, and it can be changed permanently. Moreover, there are women wrestlers and weight lifters and male nurses and secretaries. Very confusing.

Age doesn't work either. Sometimes, you just can't tell. Anyway, old people have the money, young people have the fun, and middle-aged people have the power. The cost of alienating any one group is just too high.

But human height meets all of the core criteria:

- Everybody has one.
- It can be seen at a distance.
- It is decided at birth and difficult to alter by more than a few inches.
- A medium-sized majority can be easily established.
- It is completely arbitrary, having nothing to do with anything of real value.

Moreover, everybody can play: Tall people can look down on short people as physically inferior; short people can look down on tall people as monstrous freaks who consume far too much space and resources; and the medium-sized majority can look down on both as fringe abnormalities. Better yet, height can be measured with precision, it cannot be altered by prolonged exposure to the sun, and the majority can be maintained over time simply by raising or lowering boundaries as necessary.

Nothing lasts forever. One of these days, the news about how Tiger Woods and Halle Berry were conceived may get out and same-race marriages will be dead forever. Even if the story can be kept under wraps, racial prejudice is rapidly running out of majority. If we are to continue to hold the human race well below its potential, then we need a replacement and we need it fast. Luckily, human height meets every criterion: It is easily seen, it is completely arbitrary, a majority can be maintained in perpetuity—and it elevates human stupidity to a yet another high.

A Trick of Perspective

*"For now we see through a glass darkly;
but then face to face."*

—CORINTHIANS 13:12

Cecilia Sharpe has two aunts who live back east in Chewelah, which is north of Spokane. Named Flora and Fauna, they were born fraternal twins but grew up to be just about as similar as salt and soda pop.

Fauna, the elder of Cecilia's twin aunts, is a career skeptic and pessimist. She first acquired her disposition for the dark side when her fiancé lost his life at Inchon, South Korea, and later honed it in the halls of Chewelah High, where she taught world and American history for some thirty-five years.

Even though she has since retired to a comfortable life of gardening and CNN International, Fauna still feels compelled to share her peculiar historical perspective at almost every opportunity. This is especially true when a young lady is in attendance, which is the case several times each year when Cecilia and Gwendolyn come to Sunday lunch at the house of Flora and Fauna.

Typically, Gwen dreads the requisite afternoon at her great-aunts' house, despite the ever-cheerful presence of her aunt Flora, because Aunt Fauna's perspectives have a certain repetitiveness and a skew to them that she finds discomforting. But this time, with her mother's complicity and the assistance of a recent edition of *The Economist Pocket World in Figures*, Gwen had prepared a riposte.

Luncheon, which consisted of an excellent pork roast with baked apples and fresh corn on the cob, was filled with small talk, as if everyone were avoiding the inevitable. Afterward, the four women repaired to the sitting room for coffee and tea. They had not been sipping for long when Fauna, who had never married, mentioned that she had recently heard on television that Americans had the highest divorce rate in the world and that, as a direct result, marriage as an institution was doomed to insignificance.

Flora picked up her latest knitting project and began working quietly. Cecilia smiled politely. Gwendolyn, who was a graduate student in anthropology, checked her figures and then replied that the United States also had the tenth-highest marriage rate in the world and that the net marriage rate, which was marriages less divorces, was near the world average.

Undaunted, Fauna blamed the unprecedented divorce rate on the high cost of living and the necessity for both spouses to work to make ends meet. But, according to Gwen's *Pocket World in Figures*, the purchasing power of the average U.S. citizen was the second-highest in the world, trailing only Luxembourg, and more than 20 percent greater than that of the Japanese, the Germans, the

French, the English, and the Canadians. She added that average buying power in the United States was more than twice that in Greece, South Korea, and Portugal, more than four times that of the average Mexican, and more than thirty times the purchasing power of citizens in a dozen African nations.

Like Macduff, Fauna redoubled her efforts. Glancing at the six-year-old Honda in their driveway, she observed that the cost of automobiles was still beyond the reach of most Americans. Gwendolyn answered that there was more than one car for every two Americans, the second-highest automotive ownership rate in the world and more than 50 percent higher than the Japanese. In comparison, some twenty-nine countries in the world, including China, managed to get by with less than one car for every 200 citizens.

Fauna sighed, looked over at Flora, who was purling in the corner and humming softly, and then suggested that the excessive rate of automobile ownership might explain why the roads were so crowded, especially in downtown Spokane. Gwendolyn nodded sympathetically, but then added that the U.S. road system was more than three times larger than that of any other nation in the world, more than five times larger than Russia's, Japan's, China's, and Canada's, and more than fifteen times as large as the United Kingdom's.

Fauna replied that lax immigration laws had caused the United States to become far too crowded. But Gwendolyn checked her *Pocket World in Figures* and discovered that Germany, the United Kingdom, and Japan were eight to eleven times as densely populated as the United States.

Cecilia could see that her aunt was showing signs of distress, so she suggested that they take a break. Fauna, however, noted that she had little time left at her age and she intended to enjoy it with her relatives. Feeling a release from years of repetitive pessimism abuse, Gwen instantly responded that Fauna, who was sixty-five years old, could expect to live at least another twenty years, whereas had she been born in any of forty other countries in the world, it was likely that she would have already been dead for ten years or more.

Fauna shook her head, then stood to leave the room. Cecilia asked her to stay. Flora knitted. Gwendolyn said nothing. Fauna surveyed the room slowly, then remarked that, given the deteriorating quality of life in the United States, another twenty years might not be that much of a blessing.

Before Cecilia could intervene, Gwen replied that, according to a U.N. measurement that combined income level, literacy, and life expectancy (and not the weather), the United States had the second-highest quality of life in the world, trailing only Canada.

Fauna muttered something about packing for the move up north and left the room. Cecilia looked sternly at Gwen, who, despite her victory, had begun to fiddle nervously with her *World in Figures*. Flora, who had traveled extensively in her younger years, finished a stitch and looked up for the first time in nearly half an hour. Smiling, she told Cecilia and Gwen that, in more than six decades of existence, Fauna had never crossed an American border. As long as she didn't, she would never have to confront the opinions she had so carefully formed in isolation. Thus, they would remain, until her demise, a trick of perspective.

34

The Importance of Small Infinities

> *"To see a world in a grain of sand*
> *And Heaven in a wild flower*
> *Hold infinity in the palm of your hand*
> *And eternity in an hour."*

—WILLIAM BLAKE

Flora Sharpe, Fauna's younger twin and polar opposite, has been a hairdresser and a card-carrying optimist since grade school. Despite her advanced age and more physical imperfections than a Russian nuclear power plant, she still stands all day, six days per week, fixing hair at Flora's Salon de Coiffure up on Cozy Nook Road in Chewelah.

On a late Sunday afternoon last summer, Flora fixed Cecilia's hair, which was badly in need of a cut and some color, while Gwen reminisced with her *Pocket World in Figures* in an alcove next to the front window. Flora hummed, rather badly, as she worked. So, about two minutes into the cut, Cecilia asked Flora why she had chosen a career in hairdressing. Before the sun had set in the west on that fine, cloudless day, Cecilia understood the importance of small infinities.

Flora, it turned out, had always yearned for a career in the arts. Her first choice was architecture. Unfortunately, she learned in the third grade that she was both nearsighted and color-blind. Since she couldn't draw a straight line anyway, the life of an architect or a landscape artist seemed out of the question.

Undaunted, young Flora tried her hand at music. But she had a tin ear, and her hands, although functional, had been malformed during gestation, leaving her fingers barely half the length of her sister's. So Flora's earnest attempts at the piccolo, the piano, and the bassoon produced some personal satisfaction but no practical prospect of a career.

Next, she took up dance. Sadly, though, the deformity that affected Flora's fingers also affected her toes, and therefore her balance. And although she could boogie with the best in Stevens County, Flora was short and built not at all like a Rockette.

A less committed woman might have settled for a career in county politics, but Flora was an artist. So she took up writing. Alas, her dyslexia, which predated the invention of the spell checker by some fifty years, proved to be a serious handicap. Besides, her parents could afford to send only one daughter to college, and that had to be Fauna, who was more talented and who aspired to teach.

Thus, every door to a career in art seemed to have been slammed shut by handicap or misfortune. However, although more things go wrong, not everything does. One day while Flora was walking home from high school, she happened to pass by a new hair salon in the neighborhood. She stopped to peer in the window and remained there for a long time, so long that the proprietress invited her in to watch firsthand.

Flora and the hairdresser became fast friends, then Flora began to work part-time in the salon. As a helper, she quickly learned that every head of hair was different and that there was an infinity of styles, cuts, and colors for each one. As an apprentice, she learned that her hands were more than strong enough to manage the tools of the art, especially after her experience with the bassoon. And, as a full-fledged hairdresser, she learned that she had the ability to uplift her clientele with an innovative cut, an inspired perm, or an unusual story about the branch of her family that had gone over the mountains to Seattle.

Flora had found her small infinity—and a career in art, in coiffure. In fact, there is a small infinity in an individual strand of hair. Each one is always growing and always changing. It can never be in exactly the same place twice. It can be shortened, straightened, curled, or dyed an endless array of colors. If it falls out, it usually grows back, but differently. If they all fall out, then there is always another head of hair.

In the same way, there is a small infinity in a leaf on a tree, in a cloud in the sky, and in the movements of the pieces on a chessboard. Likewise, there is a small if somewhat grander infinity in gardening, in meteorology, and in competitive chess.

The lesson was not lost on Cecilia, who had a career but no real hobby. Knowing that the responsibilities of motherhood would be behind her too soon, Cecilia resolved to find a small infinity of interest that would outlast both her maternal duties and her work.

Cecilia, like most of us, does not have to face the physical handicaps that had to be overcome by Flora. However, Nature provides all of us with frailties or weaknesses from birth. As we age, our infirmities accumulate in number and increase in degree, diminishing our ability to experience the full breadth of life.

In return, however, Nature provides us all with an endless supply of small infinities. Each small infinity can be, in itself, an inexhaustible reservoir of unique experience, personal expression, and boundless exploration. Regardless of our state of health, we can never see it all or smell it all or say it all or sew it all or solve it all or sail it all or sink them all. In every small infinity, one of which is the universe of numbers, there is always more.

But perhaps the greatest of all small infinities is the written word. More is being published each day than can be read in any lifetime. Books, newspapers, magazines, and the Internet are an open doorway to every form of experience—past and present, sensory and philosophical, sensible and fantastic. By reading what we can, each of us can survey the known universe of small infinities and choose what we wish to experience firsthand. The right choices can lead to a career, or a passion, or a moment, that will last a lifetime.

Life after Death

*"If a man has a strong faith he can indulge
in the luxury of skepticism."*

—FRIEDRICH WILHELM NIETZSCHE

The question of life after death has persevered through the ages for at least two reasons:

1. From a personal perspective, the stakes are rather high.
2. The usual answer, although reassuring, is not certain. In Western culture, only one person is widely believed to have died and come back to tell about the afterlife; it was a long time ago, and His report remains uncorroborated by others of similar stature.

It is possible that Nature invented life and death this way on purpose. As long as there is uncertainty in death, then each life must be lived to its fullest. So a firm answer to the question "Is there life after death?" may forever be beyond mortal proof. But even within the confines of secular experience, we have accumulated an abundance of clues.

Every time a new, more powerful telescope is applied to the exploration of space, more is discovered. Every time a more powerful particle accelerator is applied to the study of subatomic constructs, more is uncovered. New forms of life are being identified all the time, from the past, from the present, possibly even from space. We have even learned that matter is not always matter. Particles can become waves and vice versa, and there is something else called "Dark Matter." And the advancement of mathematics predicts much more: as many as ten dimensions of existence.

It appears that our universe really is infinitely large, infinitesimally small, and incomprehensibly complex. Everywhere man explores, there is always more.

What, then, is the probability that mankind is the sole exception to this Law of Nature, the "Rule of Always More"? What if, in this one case, all we are is what we can see?

If the total number of cases that fall under the "Rule of Always More" is infinite, as it appears to be so far, then the probability that mankind is the sole example to the contrary is one divided by infinity. One over infinity is as close to zero as you can get without actually getting there. Thus, the "Rule of Always More" seems to be telling us that there are more dimensions of scale and complexity to our own existence than we can ever know in this life.

We also know that Nature conserves everything. No molecule, no atom, no electron, no photon is ever lost because of a change in state. Instead, it is converted into energy, a wave, or some other form of existence. If death is a change of state, as it seems to be, then what we see of ourselves, and what we can't see, must also be conserved after the change. The conservation of what we can't see would seem necessarily to include personality. Even so, we could be more confident if there were another way to infer that individual identity is preserved after death.

However, just to be contrarian, let's assume that identity is not conserved after death. Then we must also accept that every single sighting of every human apparition, literally millions of them across the history of man, has been a fabrication. But is it possible that everyone who has ever claimed to see a ghost was a liar or delusional?

Let's assume that only a million people have claimed to have seen a ghost over the entirety of human history, which seems conservatively low, and that 99.99 percent of all such sightings were either delusional or just made up, which seems cautiously high. Then, over the entire 5,000-year course of recorded history, just one hundred people (0.01 percent of one million) have observed a genuine afterlife existence. But that is precisely 100 times as many as necessary, because it takes exactly one legitimate afterlife encounter to prove the point. (Solely on the basis of this model, the inference of life after death is still intact at a prevarication rate of 99.9999 percent.)

Moreover, if there is no life after death, Nature is also on the con. If our identity is not preserved after death, then why can some of us be transported back to previous lives through hypnosis? Is all of that information not really stored in the brain? Can it be just an extemporaneous creation of the mind, or a preprogrammed fantasy—every single time?

And what are we to make of the consistency of reports of

the life-after-death experience: the sense of warmth and well-being, the white light, the reception by past loved ones? If we assume that there is no life after death, then we must conclude that each of these experiences, each and every one, is either a fabrication or, perhaps, some sort of "exit routine" to ease our demise.

Software engineers, by the way, create exit routines to preserve the wholeness and working order of their computer programs so that they can be reused—at another time, in another computer, or in case of an abnormal ending. Maybe Nature has wasted a lot of brain capacity on a useless "exit routine." But as far as we know, Nature doesn't waste anything. So perhaps our "programs" are "saved" at death for another container. The Dalai Lama, the leader of the Buddhist religion and the lawful ruler of Tibet, should be happy to provide some spiritual support to this theory. He is, after all, believed to have returned from the dead thirteen times in different incarnations.

But reincarnation is religion, so it may be concoction. Then again, perhaps we can find our immortality in the science of concoction.

For many, many years, astrophysicists were troubled by the math of the Big Bang, that primordial explosion that started all of this so long ago. In a nutshell, there just wasn't enough matter in the universe to allow galaxies to form, at least according to the theories of a rather highly regarded physicist named Isaac Newton. That meant one of three things:

1. That Newton, despite three hundred years of evidence to the contrary, was wrong.
2. That the Milky Way never really existed.

3. That there was more matter out there than scientists could detect.

Luckily for Newton and the rest of us, the astrophysicists chose option three. So they concocted something called Dark Matter, which cannot be seen but which they hypothesized to comprise some 90 percent of the mass of the known universe. Once they did, the integrity of Newtonian physics was restored. In the few years since then, although it still can't be seen, firm evidence of Dark Matter has indeed been discovered. The "Rule of Always More," it seems, even applies to things we cannot see or touch.

Either our personalities are the only known exception to Nature's Law of Conservation, or there is life after death. Either every past-life experience in the history of man has been an invention, or there is life after death. Either every life-after-life experience has been an illusion, or there is life after death. Either every paranormal experience has been a delusion, or there is life after death. Either every religion has been a concoction, Jesus did not return from the dead, and the Dalai Lama has never come back at all, much less thirteen times, or there is life after death. Either mankind is the only known exception to the "Rule of Always More," or there is life after death.

In this accumulation of experience and inference, we may be reasonably confident that there is life after death. But only the devout may be certain of it. The rest of us, like those enlightened scientists who "invented" Dark Matter, will have to await corroboration.

Are We Alone?

"I don't believe there's no sich a person."

—CHARLES DICKENS

Thousands, perhaps millions, believe that they have seen incontrovertible evidence of alien intelligence in the skies over planet Earth. But no respected government body, including NASA and the U.S. Air Force, has ever produced hard evidence to support these observations.

Despite the lack of hard evidence, it is impractical in the extreme to prove that we are alone. The only meticulous method would be to visit every planet in every solar system in every galaxy in the universe, assuming this is the only universe. And despite the rather obvious expense and time consumption, even this could prove to be inconclusive.

Since 1993, NASA scientists have been analyzing a rock, playfully nicknamed ALH, that was found in the Antarctic but is believed to have dropped in originally from Mars. It has small, bacteria-like constructs in it that look as if they may have once been a primitive form of life. Some scientists apparently believe this, others disagree, some are on the fence awaiting more data, and some aren't even sure that the rock came from Mars. However, even if low forms of past life on Mars are eventually proven (the rock is billions of years old), the question of intelligent life, which is an entirely different matter, will probably continue to persist for many, many years.

Back in 1961, a group of prominent scientists decided that they couldn't wait anymore. So they got together at the National Radio Astronomy Observatory at Green Bank, West Virginia, to see if they could build some sort of model that would predict the probability of intelligent extraterrestrial life. They came up with a simple equation, now commonly referred to in astronomical circles as the Green Bank or Drake Equation, that attempts to estimate the probable number of planets in the Milky Way (our galaxy) that can support intelligent life. The equation is:

$$N = R^* \times f_p \times n_e \times f_l \times f_i \times f_c \times L; \text{ where}$$

N = the number of planets with intelligent life in the Milky Way

R^* = the mean rate of star formation in the Milky Way

f_p = the fraction of those stars which form planetary systems

n_e = the number of planets in those systems that are ecologically suitable for life

f_l = the probability that life-forms actually develop on those planets

f_i = the probability that intelligent life evolves on those planets

fc = the probability that advanced, technical
civilizations also develop
L = the estimated lifetime, in years, of those advanced
technical civilizations

Although controversial, the values for each parameter
that was initially put forward were: $R^* = 10$ per year;
$fp = 0.5$; $ne = 2$; $fl = 1$; $fi \times fc = 0.01$; and $L = 10$. That
means that N, the number of planets that support intelligent life in our galaxy, equals:

$$10 \times .5 \times 2 \times 1 \times 0.01 \times 10 = 1.$$

Thus, the Drake Equation would seem to conclude that
we, as human beings, are in an intellectual league of our
own in the Milky Way. However, the value of each of the
unknowns in the equation has always been speculative, especially L (the peak lifetime of advanced, technical civilizations), which was forecast in 1961, the peak of the Cold
War, to be a paltry ten years. Now, of course, we know that
we are much more likely to destroy ourselves through pol-
lution and overpopulation, which will probably take longer
than ten years (although anything is possible).

If, for instance, we were only to increase the value of L to
100 years, then the Drake Equation would forecast a total of
ten planets in the Milky Way that could support intelligent
life. Carl Sagan, in fact, predicted that the number of planets
supporting intelligent life could be more than 100, which
does not seem to be a gross exaggeration in a single galaxy of
some 200,000,000,000 stars. More recently, Frank Drake,
the principal architect of the Drake Equation, has increased
his estimate from 10,000 to as many as 100,000.

But there's another factor to consider. The age of the universe, and our galaxy, has been estimated by Stephen Hawking and others to be around 15,000,000,000 years, give or take five billion. Thus, even if there have been 10,000 intelligent civilizations in the Milky Way, and even if each of them thrived for 10,000 years, then it would seem unlikely that an extraterrestrial civilization in our galaxy would exist at the same time as ours (10,000 times 10,000 is 100 million, which is just 1 percent of 10 billion).

Once again, it seems likely that we are alone in the Milky Way. However, there are lots of other galaxies. Based upon recent data from the Hubble telescope, NASA estimates the number of galaxies in the known universe to be at least fifty billion. Assuming that our galaxy is average, then this would seem to predict that the number of planets capable of supporting advanced, intelligent life forms in the universe could be as low as fifty billion, which is the original Green Bank estimate of one per galaxy (ours) times the estimated number of galaxies. On the other hand, it could be more than 500 trillion, which is the low end of the more recent Drake estimate of 10,000 such planets in our galaxy times 50 billion galaxies.

At this point, we pretty much ought to concede either that the entire universe was constructed for us alone, which means that billions of galaxies with billions of stars in each one are all currently without any television whatsoever; or we should conclude that there are millions, if not billions or trillions, of other planets in the universe that are capable of supporting intelligent civilizations, some of whom, if they are close enough (within forty-five light-years or so), could be watching original transmissions of *The Mickey Mouse Club* at this very moment.

The real difficulty may be in getting from our little out-post of life to their little outpost, or vice versa. If the closest surviving extraterrestrial civilization is somewhere in Andromeda, which is the galaxy nearest to our own, then we will need to traverse about 2.2 million light-years of space in order to visit our neighbors. A light-year is the distance that light travels in a year, which is approximately 5.88 billion miles. If our spacecraft travels at an average of 100,000 miles per second (which is about 54 percent of the speed of light and which would get us to the moon in around 2.4 seconds) on its voyage to Andromeda, it will get there in around 4.1 million years. Then it would take another 2.2 million years for the news of contact to get back to Earth.

Any alien civilization desiring to travel to planet Earth would have to confront the same distance and time problem, unless they have figured out how to travel faster than the speed of light. Based upon what we know today, though, the speed of light cannot be exceeded. Moreover, the closer one comes to it, the heavier he or she becomes, which means that an impatient space traveler could develop an infinitely serious weight problem.

Until we contact a species from another planet, or until an alien race contacts us, we cannot know for certain that there is life elsewhere in the universe. And the distances in the universe are so vast that the proof of the existence of extraterrestrial intelligence may be many, many years, per-haps even millions of years, in the future.

This uncertainty may be provident. Because the dis-tances of space are so vast, and because the limitations of what we currently know of physics are so rigid, it appears that our species has been given plenty of time, those same millions of years, to manage our own evolution without risk of external intervention.

Maybe that is, after all, the Divine Intention: that no race may contact another until it has proven that it can survive on its own for millions of years. Then again, there is periodic but unconfirmed evidence that Earth has been visited by an advanced alien race. If so, they were probably in search of intelligent life. It appears, however, that they have since departed, possibly due to insufficient evidence.

37

A Message from Rapa Nui

"I shall have more to say when I am dead."

—EDWARD ARLINGTON ROBINSON

Sometime around 400 A.D., seafaring Polynesians discovered the island of Rapa Nui in the South Pacific. Although Rapa Nui was more than two thousand miles from the nearest civilization, which made trade impossible, human life flourished there. The weather was almost perfect. There was abundant fresh water, and the volcanic topsoil, although lacking depth, was very fertile. At that time, much of the island was covered with a biologically diverse forest, the tallest indigenous species of which were palm trees that may have grown to more than eighty feet in height and six feet in diameter. Under the forest canopy, there was an abundance of plants and wildlife, including more than thirty species of fowl. And, although the island lacked easy access to large quantities of tropical fish like so much of the South Pacific, there was an almost limitless supply of deepwater porpoise reachable by canoe.

Over the next thousand years, the population of the remote island rose to somewhere between four thousand and ten thousand inhabitants. But in the process of converting their raw, isolated paradise into a suitable human habitat, the tribes of Rapa Nui deforested the island. Rain and wind destroyed the exposed topsoil. Water resources and the supply of game and fowl were depleted. Because there were no more trees of sufficient size, canoes disappeared, making the fish supply inaccessible and escape impossible.

Thus, the people of Rapa Nui became trapped in an increasingly inhospitable environment of their own construction. As resources became even more scarce, the tribes resorted to warfare. Eventually they fell into cannibalism, and civilization on the island collapsed, just as its ecology had. By the time the island was "discovered" by the Dutch ship captain Jakob Roggeveen, on Easter Day in 1722, the population had crashed to less than two thousand. The remaining inhabitants of Rapa Nui were poor and hungry, eking out a miserable living on what was left of the land and what they could eat of each other.

Naturally, a burgeoning slave trade and the inevitable arrival of European missionaries accelerated the destruction of the island, including the written and spoken records of its fall from ecological grace. By the year 1900, there were only 111 people left on Rapa Nui, which, by that time, had been renamed Easter Island.

Gwendolyn Sharpe arrived on Rapa Nui almost a hundred years later. She did not come to see the famous *moai*, the great stone statues, some as tall as thirty-three feet and weighing as much as eighty-two tons, that rim the ancient island. Instead, like so many anthropologists of modern times, she came to study the rise and fall of the civilization of Rapa Nui. But Gwendolyn quickly discovered that the great statues played a prominent role in the island's sad tale.

The *moai* were quarried by the tribes of Rapa Nui in a caldera near the center of the island. They then had to be moved, one at a time, to their final observation posts on the island's rim, as much as fourteen miles away. Since they were so large and so heavy, the process of moving them became, by necessity, an even greater engineering achievement than their creation. By using the island's large, indigenous palm trees like bearings, the *moai* were actually "skateboarded" to their final destination, possibly standing up.

Over time, in what was apparently a sort of tribal competition that had been empowered by palm tree transportation technology, the *moai* became larger and larger. Hence, the moving process required more and more palm trees, just as the growing population required more and more land to farm.

Today, there are no great palm trees on Rapa Nui. There haven't been for more than three hundred years, and they aren't growing back. The people of Rapa Nui cut them all down. Every one. No forest canopy, no wildlife. No forest, no topsoil. No topsoil, no crops. No palm trees, no canoes. No canoes, no fish. No food, cannibalism.

Like any other sentient person who has encountered the story of Rapa Nui, Gwendolyn wondered at its portent. Unlike most others, however, Gwen was the daughter of an accountant. So she took out her Sharp (no relation) calculator and cut a few numbers:

- First, she calculated the total landmass of Rapa Nui to be sixty-four square miles.
- Second, she averaged the high and low estimates of Rapa Nui's maximum population, which was thought to be between four thousand and ten thousand, to come up with a midpoint estimate of seven thousand people at the peak of the island's development.
- Third, she divided 7,000 by 64 to get 109.375, the maximum number of people per square mile, that the isolated island of Rapa Nui was apparently able to support on its own.
- Fourth, Gwendolyn got out her almanac and discovered that the entire landmass of an isolated, near paradise called planet Earth is 52,433,000 square miles, excluding Antarctica.
- Fifth, and nervously, Gwen multiplied 52,433,000 square miles by 109.375 to get a theoretical maximum world population of 5,734,859,000 human beings.
- Finally, via satellite, Gwen got onto the Internet and dialed into the world population clock that is maintained by the United Nations. At that moment, the world's population was 5,900,000,000 people, or 112.5 per square mile, 103 percent of the population density that had been unsupportable on the island of Rapa Nui.

Gwen took a deep breath and considered what she had discovered. On the one hand, Polynesian culture at the middle of the second millennium did not have any of the modern advances that we take for granted today—processes, technologies, and fertilizers that have multiplied the productivity of agriculture by many times. And the people of contemporary times are not preoccupied with the construction and transportation of massive stone statues.

On the other hand, although Rapa Nui is volcanic, its land was not otherwise consumed by massive deserts, or urban sprawl, or great tundras like those of Russia and Canada. And the resources of their island were not consumed by the trappings of modernization: trillions of sheets of paper, billions of electric appliances, millions of internal combustion engines, thousands of power plants.

Gwen, who had just recently believed that she had a life expectancy of more than ninety years, found herself becoming distressed. However, before she could conclude that planet Earth had exceeded a population level that it could predictably sustain without war or catastrophe, she looked for corroborating evidence. There she found:

a) destruction of the rain forests;
b) depletion of the ozone layer;
c) widespread famine and disease in Africa and elsewhere;
d) global warming; and
e) extinction of the Earth's animal and plant life at the rate of forty to sixty species *per day!*

Right then and there, Gwen should have concluded that the Earth was reaching the end of its ecological tether. However, she knew that estimates of the peak sustainable population of Rapa Nui ran as high as 10,000, which was 156.25 per square mile and more than 38 percent higher than the world's current population density. So, in one last grasp at optimism, she decided to cruise through the Web site of the United Nations Population Information Network before she logged off the Internet. There, she discovered that the U.N. predicts that the world's population will reach 8.2 billion in the year 2030, which is about 156.3 people per square mile.

Gwen also learned that the world's population is predicted to level off at 11.6 billion sometime around the year 2200. That is a density of more than 220 per square mile and approximately two times the population that was demonstrably incapable of surviving on the remote, near paradise of Rapa Nui.

Today, largely due to annexation by Chile and a tourism economy created by the mystery of the *moai*, there are two thousand people again living on the island, which is only about thirty per square mile. But there are still no forests on Rapa Nui. There are no Easter Island palms. There is also no agriculture of significance. The island of Rapa Nui has become a sparsely populated dependency fed by imports, which are paid for by tourists, who come to see the great stone symbols of its destruction.

Most of the *moai*, by the way, were still standing in the late 1700s. Over the next three or four generations, though, the citizens of Rapa Nui pulled them down. Maybe they finally got the message.

After Math:
Why More Things
Go Wrong

*"Of all human ills, greatest is fortune's
wayward tyranny."*

—SOPHOCLES

During difficult times such as these, you may be inclined
to conclude that the world is against you. That, however, would be an incorrect conclusion. The world is not
against you; Nature is. And it is personal.

The essence of Nature is an infinity of possibilities. At
any given point at any given time for any given action, an
incalculable number of distinct things can happen next. For
the most part, this is good news. Over the long run, the
principle of infinite possibilities has been essential to the
creation, diversity, and mystery of life.

But day-to-day human existence is just a bit different.
An infinity of possibilities does not always work to our advantage. That's because there is usually only a finite set of
things that can go right. In fact, we human beings tend to
define things that way. For instance, when the lawn mower

201

is working, one thing is going right. But when the lawn mower is not working, one or more things have gone wrong.

Although we can define the things that we want to go right, we cannot limit the behavior of Nature by similar definition. Instead, Nature requires that there always will be an infinite number of things that can happen next. Among the infinite number of things that can happen next, most will not affect you. Some, however, will. Among them, there is always a number of things that can go wrong. Unfortunately, this number is also infinitely large.

Anyone who has ever taken a lawn mower out of the garage for the first grass cutting of spring understands this problem. There is one right condition: The lawn mower works. Somehow, though, over the course of winter, one or more things have gone wrong: The spark plug has been fouled, the wire from the spark plug to the engine will no longer carry the spark, the gasoline tank has inexplicably taken in water, all of the oil has mysteriously turned into black goo, the plastic throttle has broken, the throttle cable has rusted to the point where it can no longer convey changes to the carburetor, the gas can has disappeared, the blade has become duller than C-Span, et cetera, et cetera, et cetera.

This is the Lawn Mower Principle. It states that there is usually one thing that can go right, but there are an infinite number of things that can happen, so there must be an infinite number of things that can go wrong. (It could just as easily be called the "First Law of Golf," because it is a principle that all golfers immediately grasp.)

The Lawn Mower Principle works everywhere, not just in the yard. In theory, for instance, business travelers can reach their destination on time. However, it rarely happens in real life: The plane arrives late to the gate because of traffic control delays, boarding is delayed while a connecting flight clears traffic control, passenger loading takes too long because the flight attendants have to check seventeen of the new carry-on steamer trunks, pullback is delayed because the In-Flight Kitchen has failed to include the required number of Kosher pasta salads, luggage is lost, flights are canceled, and airports are closed due to fog, snow, earthquake, or the arrival of Air Force One.

By the Lawn Mower Principle, there are many more things that can go wrong than can go right. Therefore, it is our job in life to act to limit the likelihood of negative outcomes and to increase the probability of a positive outcome. Without question, the most serious negative outcome that we have to limit is the probability of our extinction. According to those who study the evolution of our planet for a living, about 99.9 percent of all of the species that have ever inhabited the Earth are now extinct.

We would all like to believe that we humans are different; that our chances of survival are something better than 1,000 to one. In more than a million years of existence, we have already survived lions, tigers, and bears, Ice Ages, volcanic eruptions, earthquakes, tsunamis, tornadoes, hurricanes, floods, drought, famine, plague, pestilence, war, and the invasion of British rock and roll.

But more things will go wrong. More than 90 percent of all existing species may fail to survive the next million years. If we are to avoid their fate, then we will have to evolve. However, successful evolution in the Information Age will be very different from what it was in the Stone Age. In this new age and in each age after it, our survival will depend less on our willingness to fight and more on our courage to do what is right.

In this vital endeavor, arithmetic tells us:

- That each of us is one and the rest are many.
- That now is infinitely short and the future is infinitely long.
- That a single act of reason is more valuable than a thousand acts of ignorance.

Intelligence is not just a gift; it's a choice. Make it and evolve.